Brandscaping

Worlds of Experience in
Retail Design | Erlebnisdesign
für Einkaufswelten

Brandscaping

Worlds of Experience in Retail Design | Erlebnisdesign für Einkaufswelten

Edited by | Herausgegeben von Otto Riewoldt

Birkhäuser – Publishers for Architecture | Verlag für Architektur
Basel · Boston · Berlin

Otto Riewoldt

Brandscaping

Staging brand experiences
through architecture and interior design
Markenerlebnisse inszenieren
in Architektur und Innenarchitektur

The brand-building impact of corporate architecture has not suddenly appeared overnight. Back in the 1920s, Peter Behrens designed an expressionist gateway for the Frankfurt headquarters of chemical company Hoechst and found he had built the brand logo of the day. In Turin, the Fiat Lingotto plant had an oval racetrack laid out on the roof. Born of the futuristic spirit of the age captured by architect Giacomo Matte-Trucco, the plant stood for the dynamic elan of the brand. And in Switzerland, well aware of the symbolic impact of corporate identity set in bricks and mortar, in 1876 the Feldschlösschen ("field castle") brewery built a production facility complete with towers and battlements in a picturesque setting, lending tangible form to the brand.

Even in the past, the focus was invariably on adding value: the functional buildings required to meet a company's industrial purpose were raised to the status of symbols. Current developments go further still, with architecture and interior design becoming primary instruments of customer-oriented brand communication in their own right. Brandscaping – the three-dimensional design of brand settings – is all about forging backdrops for experiences with a high entertainment value, from flagship stores to corporate theme parks, from customized, modular shop systems to innovative mall concepts.

So neu ist der Marken bildende Beitrag von Unternehmensarchitektur nicht. Der von Peter Behrens für den Chemiekonzern Hoechst in den Zwanzigerjahren entworfene expressionistische Torbau des Frankfurter Verwaltungsgebäudes schaffte es seinerzeit, zum Markenlogo zu werden. Die aus futuristischem Geist geborene Turiner Fiat-Fabrik Linggotto des Architekten Giacomo Matte-Trucco von 1920 war mit ihrem ovalen, auf dem Dach angelegten Rennkurs Sinnbild für Dynamik und Elan der Marke. Auch der Schweizer Bieranbieter Feldschlösschen wusste um die Bildmächtigkeit gebauter Unternehmensidentität, als er seine 1876 gegründete Brauerei mit Zinnen und Türmen bewehrt in die malerische Landschaft setzte und damit dem Markennamen fassliche Gestalt gab.

Immer ging es dabei um einen Zusatznutzen: Für den industriellen Geschäftszweck notwendige Funktionsbauten wurden aufgewertet zu Symbolen. Heute indessen verselbstständigen sich Architektur und Innenarchitektur und werden zu primären Instrumenten kundenbezogener Markenkommunikation. Brandscaping, die dreidimensionale Gestaltung von Markenlandschaften, bezeichnet Erlebnisräume mit hohem Unterhaltungswert, vom Flagshipstore bis zum Corporate Theme Park, von maßgeschneiderten, modularen Shop-Systemen bis zu innovativen Mall-Konzepten.

Harnessing brandpower

In the increasingly global competition for the customer's eye, wallet and above all, heart, brands are the number-one success factor. In the consumer's consciousness they stand for values, send out powerful signals, communicate images and promise to provide the key to new experiences. Today, brands have become important landmarks. As American writer Naomi Klein rightly notes, we increasingly define our identity through the brands we choose. "Brands are the main source of identity. The brand fills a vacuum and forms a kind of armour, taking over the part once played by political, philosophical or religious ideas. Logos are becoming fetishes." Brands signal our membership of an 'in' group. They are the tools with which we build status. They ensure we belong and give us security. Brands build emotions, promise happiness and provide kicks.

The decisive paradigm shift has taken place on the emotional plane of the brand experience. Traditional forms of addressing the customer will no longer suffice if a company is to hold its own in a multimedia, globalized marketplace. The new quality of the brand experience is founded on direct interaction and a characteristic encounter. What we have here is the paradoxical phenomenon that, by enabling and anchoring immediate brand experiences, the IT age has actually upgraded the physical location. We are not talking about virtual non-experiences in the no-mans-land of the Internet, but about concrete encounters in real locations, where the world of the brand is staged and enacted. Here, we can experience the manifestation, the messages and the emotions of the brand in company with the products themselves, in unadulterated, unusual and unique style. As a result, brandscapes are becoming more and more important in the image-building and positioning stakes and investments in brandscaping are rising.

Learning from the entertainment industry

Brandscaping transforms the brand itself into a location – an attraction. Behind all the brand-building efforts there lies the conviction that the glamour and power of the brand are the key weapons in the battle for target groups and customers. By staging the brand experience in flagship stores, shop designs or entire theme parks, companies communicate the image of the brand and imprint a characteristic atmosphere on the customer consciousness. Like tourist attractions, brands are now firmly on the map. Leading

Mythos Marke

Marken sind im internationalisierten Wettbewerb um Aufmerksamkeit, Budget und vor allem Zuneigung der Kunden der Erfolgsfaktor Nummer eins. Im Bewusstsein der Konsumenten verkörpern sie Werte, sie setzen starke Signale, sie liefern Bilder und sie suggerieren, Schlüssel zu Erlebnissen zu sein. Marken sind heute wesentliche Orientierungspunkte. Über sie definieren wir zunehmend unsere Identität, wie die US-Autorin Naomi Klein treffend feststellt: „Brands sind die Hauptquelle der Identität. Die Marke füllt ein Vakuum, bildet eine Art Schutzpanzer, der das ersetzt, was vor einiger Zeit noch politische, philosophische oder religiöse Ideen waren. Logos werden zu Fetischen." Marken vermitteln Zugehörigkeit zu einer In-Group, sie wirken als Statusinstrumente, sie garantieren Bindung und Sicherheit. Marken schaffen Emotionen, sie sind Glücksverheißung und Stimmungsgeber.

Der entscheidende Paradigmenwechsel hat sich auf der emotionalen Ebene des Markenerlebnisses ereignet. Die traditionellen Formen der Kundenansprache genügen nicht mehr, um sich auf dem multimedialen, globalisierten Marktplatz zu behaupten. Die neue Qualität des Markenerlebnisses basiert auf direkter Interaktion und unverwechselbarer Erfahrung. Das paradoxe Phänomen ist eingetreten, dass das Informationszeitalter bei der Promotion und Verankerung unmittelbarer Markenerlebnisse eine Aufwertung des realen Ortes generiert. Nicht virtuell im Irgendwo und Nirgendwo von Internet oder Websites, sondern konkret an wirklichen Bezugspunkten wird die Begegnung mit der Markenwelt inszeniert. Hier ist der Markenausdruck, sind die Botschaften, Gefühle und schließlich auch die Produkte auf unverfälschte, ungewöhnliche und einmalige Weise erlebbar. Markenlandschaften erhalten daher einen immer höheren Stellenwert für Imagebildung und Positionierung, die entsprechenden Investitionen steigen.

Lernen von der Unterhaltungsindustrie

Brandscaping bedeutet, dass die Marke selbst zum Ort wird, zum Zielpunkt. Hinter der gebauten Markenidentität steht die Überzeugung, dass Glanz und Stärke der Marke im Wettstreit um Zielgruppen und Käufer entscheidend sind. Die Selbstinszenierung in Flagshipstores, Shop-Designs oder ganzen Erlebnisparks transportiert das Markenimage und vermittelt atmosphärische Erlebnisse. Die Marke setzt sich als Attraktion auf die

by example, Nike, the global market leader in sports goods, is pursuing one such concept through its NikeTowns, located at the heart of the world's most famous cities.

The borrowings from the entertainment industry are obvious in these multimedia-packed places of pilgrimage. For the perfect examples, look no further than automobile brands such as VW and BMW, who have transferred the theme park concept en bloc to their automotive worlds of experience. In the summer of 2000, the Volkswagen Group opened its 25-hectare AutoStadt (CarCity) in the immediate vicinity of its main production plant in Wolfsburg, Germany. In this theme park devoted to the four-wheeled object of desire, each of the Group's brands has its own pavilion in what is tantamount to a polytheistic place of worship, dotted with temples dedicated to the gods of the brands. Another item of customer-specific experience architecture was opened in the autumn of 2001 at the heart of historic Dresden. Here, in a 'Transparent Factory', the final assembly of the Phaeton, Volkswagen's flagship model, takes place in full public view.

The competition is now busy catching up: BMW has far more ambitious architectural plans for its "Event and Delivery Center" located directly alongside its Munich headquarters and the Olympic Park. A worldwide competition yielded exceptional results – confirming architecture's potential to create trademarks of international standing.

Omnipresent shopping

In the manifesto of the Harvard Project on the City, stewarded by architect Rem Koolhaas, it says: "Through a battery of increasingly predatory forms, shopping has been able to colonize – even replace – almost every aspect of urban life." And indeed, the omnipresence of shopping opportunities and the hybrid penetration of traditional urban structures by sales space are key characteristics of urban change. Stations mutate into shopping centres, former department stores become city malls, and in every case, the developers and operators of these complex and costly projects must spare no effort to ensure that, as attractions, these locations attain the character of fully fledged brands in their own right.

In this form of brandscaping, we are not talking about making a brand into a place but making a place into a brand. This calls for a remarkable design quality, an attractive range of tenants and a mixture of shopping, leisure

Landkarte. Exemplarisch verfolgt dieses Konzept der Weltmarktführer in Sachen Sportausrüstung Nike mit seinen NikeTowns, deren Standorte die Zentren der berühmtesten Städte rund um den Globus sind.

Unübersehbar sind schon in diesen multimedial aufgeladenen Pilgerstätten die Anleihen bei der Unterhaltungsindustrie. Das beste Beispiel dafür sind Automobilmarken wie VW und BMW, die das Schema der Vergnügungsparks auf automobile Erlebnislandschaften transferieren. Im Sommer 2000 eröffnete der VW-Konzern in unmittelbarer Nachbarschaft zu seinem Hauptwerk in Wolfsburg die 25 Hektar große AutoStadt. In diesem Themenpark rund ums vierrädrige Objekt der Begierde unterhält jede Konzernmarke ihren eigenen Pavillon, ein polytheistischer heiliger Hain mit verstreuten Tempeln für die Markengötter. Ein weiteres Stück kundenspezifischer Erlebnisarchitektur steht seit Herbst 2001 mitten im historischen Dresden: Dort wird in einer Gläsernen Manufaktur das VW-Topmodell Phaeton vor Publikum endgefertigt.

Die Konkurrenz zieht nach: Architektonisch weit ambitionierter legte BMW das Projekt seines „Erlebnis- und Auslieferungszentrums" direkt neben der Münchner Hauptverwaltung und dem Olympiagelände an. Ein weltweiter Wettbewerb brachte herausragende Ergebnisse und bestätigte damit Architektur als potenzielles Markenzeichen von internationalem Rang.

Allgegenwart Shopping

Im Manifest des vom Architekten Rem Koolhaas betreuten Harvard Project on the City heißt es: „Durch ein ganzes Arsenal zunehmend räuberischer Formen ist Shopping in der Lage, fast jeden Bereich urbanen Lebens zu kolonisieren, ja sogar zu ersetzen." Tatsächlich ist die Allgegenwart von Einkaufsgelegenheiten, die hybride Durchdringung überkommener städtischer Texturen mit Verkaufsflächen, ein wesentliches Charakteristikum des urbanen Wandels. Bahnhöfe mutieren zu Einkaufszentren, frühere Kaufhäuser zu City-Malls, und in jedem Fall müssen Entwickler und Betreiber dieser aufwändigen Projekte alles daran setzen, dass diese erfolgreich als Zielort einen eigenen genuinen Markencharakter ausbilden.

Brandscaping erfordert hier nicht, die Marke zum Ort, sondern den Ort zur Marke zu machen. Dafür braucht es eine herausragende gestalterische Qualität, eine attraktive Mieterbelegung und einen Mix aus Shopping, Freizeit, Entertainment. Ein Paradebeispiel dafür, wie man einen bekannten Ort

and entertainment. One excellent example of how a familiar location can be transformed and upgraded by adding new functions is provided by Leipzig's old main station. Completed in 1915, this piece of transport architecture is the world's largest railway terminus. Following comprehensive modernization, it can now fairly be described as the world's largest shopping centre with its own rail link. Another inner-city problem – the demise of traditional department stores – opens up new opportunities to revitalize 1A locations. In their place, new kinds of city malls are opening up which not only present the perfect catwalk for product and shop brands but also develop inherent brand qualities as attractions in their own right.

Backdrops to happiness

In his latest book, "Kulissen des Glücks" (Backdrops to Happiness), sociologist Gerhard Schulze analyses the various forms of these experience settings. "We find carefully constructed façades, filled with life by suppliers and consumers. Their raison d'être is to provide a brief experience, a short sensation of happiness." Against these backdrops to happiness, the customer becomes an actor. With the same professional care as in a theatre, each step of each scene is carefully defined, from the props to the stage directions, transforming the sale of goods into an exciting plot in which the potential customer is not so much a passive spectator as a character in the play, heading for a happy end with credit card in hand. In their book "The Experience Economy" (1999) B. Joseph Pine II and James H. Gilmore maintain that "Staging experiences is not about entertaining customers, it's about engaging them".

The primary objective is not to sell the product but to generate a fascination with the brand; to get the customer to identify with the world of the brand, creating a brand awareness and providing it with a deep-set emotional anchor. The act of purchasing becomes the potential climax. This dramatization of the brand experience calls for 'experience architecture'. Architecture and design assume a new significance in the retail sector, because as an expression of the image and message of the brand, they are a vital part of any convincing presentation. One aspect, which is becoming increasingly important here, is the dialectic between familiarity and elements of surprise. As actors, customers must encounter familiar aspects and be able to find their way around by recognizing landmarks or layouts,

durch neue Funktionen um- und aufwerten kann, verkörpert der alte Hauptbahnhof von Leipzig. Das 1915 fertig gestellte Verkehrsbauwerk ist der größte Kopfbahnhof der Welt. Nach einer umfassenden Modernisierung kann er jetzt auch den Titel der weltgrößten Einkaufsmeile mit Gleisanschluss beanspruchen. Auch ein anderes innerstädtisches Problemfeld, das Sterben der traditionellen Kaufhäuser, eröffnet Chancen zur Revitalisierung von 1-A-Lagen. Neue Typen der City-Malls entstehen, die nicht nur perfekte Laufstege für Produkt- und Shopmarken sein sollen, sondern als Attraktion selbst Markenqualität entwickeln.

Kulissen des Glücks

In seiner neuesten Veröffentlichung „Kulissen des Glücks" analysiert der Soziologe Gerhard Schulze die Erscheinungsformen inszenierter Erlebnisräume: „Es sind bewusst aufgebaute Fassaden, die von Anbietern und Konsumenten mit Leben erfüllt werden. Sie sind dazu da, ein schönes Erlebnis, ein kurzes Glücksgefühl zu erzeugen." In diesen Kulissen des Glücks wird der Kunde zum Akteur. Mit der gleichen Sorgfalt und Professionalität wie auf der Bühne müssen von der Requisite bis zur Regie die szenischen Abläufe ausgearbeitet werden, um aus dem Handel mit Waren eine erlebnisreiche Handlung zu machen, in der die potenziellen Käufer nicht nur zu passiven Zuschauern, sondern zu Rollenspielern werden, die schließlich zum Happy End ihre Kreditkarten zücken. In ihrem Buch „The Experience Economy" (1999) behaupten die Autoren B. Joseph Pine II und James H. Gilmore: „Erlebnisse inszenieren bedeutet nicht, die Kunden zu unterhalten, es geht darum, sie tatsächlich einzubeziehen."

Das Ziel heißt nicht vordergründig Produktverkauf, sondern Faszination durch die Marke, Identifikation mit der Markenwelt, Schaffung von emotional tief verankertem Markenbewusstsein. Der Kaufakt wird zur möglichen Klimax. Für diese Dramaturgie der Markenerfahrung braucht es Erlebnisarchitektur. Architektur und Design gelangen im Einzelhandel zu neuer Geltung, denn sie sind als Ausdruck von Image und Markenbotschaft unverzichtbarer Bestandteil eines überzeugenden Auftritts. Zusehends wichtiger wird hierbei die Dialektik zwischen Wiedererkennbarkeit und Überraschungsmoment. Der Kunde als Akteur muss Bekanntes wiederfinden, seine Orientierung behalten oder bestätigt finden, zugleich aber auch mit Spannung Neues erleben. Im Brandscaping sind Architektur und

but at the same time there must be exciting new elements for them to experience. In brandscaping, architecture and interior design are the stage that provides a setting for ever-changing scenes.

As the immediate environment of the brand experience, salesrooms and shopping centres themselves take on brand character. Down to the finest detail of interior design, they are geared to transmit a message that translates design into emotional impact. Hardware and soft values combine in subtle and suggestive seduction strategies that guide customers through the world of the brand and stage-manage the directions in which their attention is focused. As a success factor, the entertainment qualities of architecture and interior design play an increasingly important part in building an appropriate stage for the mercantile backdrops to happiness.

Innenarchitektur wie die Bühne Passepartout für wechselnde Inszenierungen.

Verkaufsräume oder Einkaufszentren zeigen als unmittelbare Träger des Markenerlebnisses selbst Markencharakter. Bis in jedes innenarchitektonische Detail sind sie getrimmt auf die kommunikative Botschaft, die gestalterische und emotionale Identität signalisiert. Hardware und Soft Values werden Teil subtiler, suggestiver Verführungsstrategien, die den Besucher durch die Warenwelt leiten und die Aufmerksamkeit dramaturgisch lenken. Als Erfolgsfaktor spielen die Unterhaltungsqualitäten von Architektur und Innenarchitektur als angemessener baulicher Rahmen für die merkantilen Kulissen des Glücks eine immer wesentlichere Rolle.

Postscript

The idea behind this publication was generated by an international expert workshop entitled "Brandscaping – New Dimensions of Retail Design" which was staged in Lemgo, Germany, in June 2001. The workshop was organized by the German architectural journal "Deutsche Bauzeitschrift" (Bertelsmann Fachzeitschriften Gruppe) and the lighting company Zumtobel Staff. The concluding discussions from the workshop are documented in the appendix. The editor and publishers wish to thank the organizers and participants for their support and many helpful suggestions. Also we have to express our thanks to lighting consultant Bill J. Schwinghammer, who only took part in the first part of the workshop and had to leave before the concluding discussions.

Nachbemerkung

Die Idee für die vorliegende Publikation entstammt einem internationalen Expertenworkshop, der im Juni 2001 unter dem Titel „Brandscaping – New Dimensions Of Retail Design" in Lemgo/Deutschland stattfand. Veranstalter waren die „Deutsche Bauzeitschrift" (Bertelsmann Fachzeitschriften Gruppe) und das Lichtunternehmen Zumtobel Staff. Die Abschlussdiskussion dieses Workshops ist im Anhang dokumentiert. Herausgeber und Verlag danken Veranstaltern und Teilnehmern für ihre Unterstützung und vielfältigen Anregungen. Außerdem gilt unser Dank dem Lichtdesigner Bill J. Schwinghammer, der nur am ersten Teil des Workshops, aber nicht an der Diskussion teilnehmen konnte.

STAGING BRANDS

DIE SELBST-
INSZENIERUNG
DER MARKE

Staging brands

The hardest-hitting factors in the competition for target groups and customers are the power and lustre of the brand. No one is more convinced of this key fact than the global players in the sports, fashion and automobile industries. Their investments in the bricks and mortar of their customer-oriented brand identities are on the increase. Showrooms or flagship stores alone no longer fit the bill. Temporary theme worlds or permanent theme parks form the next phase of the comprehensive brand staging process in customized experience settings. Nike, the global market leader in sports goods, is marking the mega-event of football's World Cup by opening its own spectacular "Garden of Football", while in metropolises across the globe, multimedia NikeTowns are opening up as modern-day places of pilgrimage. Upmarket mobility-maker BMW is planning a vast piece of experience architecture right alongside its Munich headquarters – a futuristic customer centre designed to make a powerful brand statement.

Die Selbstinszenierung der Marke

Was einzig zählt im Wettstreit um Zielgruppen und Käufer, sind Glanz und Stärke der Marke. Davon sind vor allem die globalen Anbieter aus Sport-, Mode- und Automobilindustrie überzeugt. Sie investieren zunehmend in ihre kundenorientierte gebaute Markenidentität. Schauräume oder Flagshipstores genügen nicht mehr: Temporäre Themenwelten oder permanente Themenparks sind die nächste Stufe der umfassenden Selbstinszenierung in Erlebnisräumen. Nike, Weltmarktführer in Sportartikeln, schlägt zu einem Megaereignis wie der Fußballweltmeisterschaft seinen eigenen spektakulären „Garden of Football" auf, in Metropolen entstehen als Pilgerstätten die multimedialen NikeTowns. BMW, Automobilhersteller im Topsegment, plant direkt neben der Münchner Hauptverwaltung ein gewaltiges Stück Erlebnisarchitektur – ein futuristisches Kundenzentrum als komprimierter Markenausdruck.

NikePark, Paris

Project | Projekt: NikePark Paris, 1998
Client | Bauherr: Nike
Creative directors | Kreativleitung: John Hoke, Greg HoffmanProject architects
Project director | Projektleiter: Chad Haws
Project manager | Projektmanager (Paris): Martine Nemecek
Production manager | Herstellungsleiter: Sara Thurman
Production manager (Retail Store) | Herstellungsleiter (Verkaufsbereich): Eric Lagrand
General contractor | Generalunternehmer: Campenon Bernard SGE
Exhibit builder | Messebau: Exhibits International
Audio/visual & lighting | AV-Technik, Lichtplanung: Satis and Fy
Retail store fixturing | Ladenbau: RTC Industries
Retail store graphics, photos | Verkaufsbereich Grafik-, Fotodesign: Capilux, P2

Design brief: Build an experience and a memory about the future of football.

The integration of football heritage with the innovation that Nike is bringing to the sport inspired the physical structures of the park. Within this environment, individuals are encouraged to take part in the football experience. Each element in the park is designed as a destination, with its own specific story to tell. Participants are encouraged to choose their own route and play out their football experience.

Big idea: The garden of football.

A new nation will claim its independence within the boundaries of Paris. It is Nike-Park, La République Populaire du Football, a place dedicated to a singular proposition – brilliant football. It is Nike's vision of football, and NikePark will promote that vision. From the players and teams it celebrates to the innovative products it will display, the park is dedicated to creating an environment that celebrates and encourages creativity, daring and spontaneous outbursts of self-expression and skill on the pitch.

Inspiration: The World's Fairs. A vision, a place, an introduction, media interest. A play on scale. Drama.

Citizens of NikePark under the age of 18 will be given a passport that entitles them to unlimited travel within the country's borders. This includes the six interactive

Entwurfsvorgabe: Baue ein Fußballerlebnis und ein Symbol für die Zukunft des Fußballs.

Die Verbindung von Fußballhistorie mit den Innovationen, die Nike für diesen Sport leistet, ist Inspiration für die Strukturierung des Parks. In dieser Umgebung werden die Besucher ermuntert, aktiver Teil des Fußballerlebnisses zu sein. Jedes Element des Parks ist als Zielpunkt gestaltet und erzählt seine eigene spezielle Geschichte. Wer hier teilnimmt, ist aufgefordert, selbst seine Wege zu wählen und sich so das individuelle Fußballerlebnis zu erspielen.

Die große Idee: der Garten des Fußballs

Eine neue Nation soll ihre Unabhängigkeit erklären innerhalb der Stadtgrenzen von Paris. Sie heißt NikePark, Volksrepublik des Fußballs. Ein Ort, der nur einer Bestimmung folgt: glanzvollem Fußball. Das ist Nikes Vision von Fußball und NikePark wirbt für diese Vision. Von den hier gefeierten Spielern und Mannschaften bis zu den ausgestellten innovativen Produkten ist der ganze Park dafür bestimmt, ein Umfeld zu schaffen, das Kreativität feiert und fördert – verwegene Ausbrüche des inneren Selbst ebenso wie Können auf dem Fußballplatz.

Inspiration: Die Weltausstellungen. Eine Vision, ein Ort, eine Einführung, Medieninteresse. Ein Spiel mit Maßstäben. Theatralik.

stations and the 1/3 scale football pitch that make up the heart of NikePark, where kids have an opportunity to experience first-hand what it means to play brilliant football.

French Park principles: Create an entry. Balance, colour, symmetry. Create a boundary. Create follies. Statues.

The park is strategically situated on the path of historic destinations, starting with the Grande Arche to the Arc de Triomphe and on to the Champs Elysées. The park becomes a part of the Paris landscape. Visitors to NikePark will also come to understand Nike's commitment to being the "total football resource". Its dedication to creating apparel, footwear and equipment to the specifications of championship athletes, and for everyone – man, woman or child – who plays and loves football. But, most important, they will leave la République Populaire du Football with the satisfaction of having experienced a place where football is not buried in strategy and tactics, but is fast and fun.

Nike Brand Design

Bürger des NikePark unter 18 Jahren werden einen Pass erhalten, der sie berechtigt, unbeschränkt innerhalb seiner Landesgrenzen zu reisen. Diese schließen sechs interaktive Stationen und das im Maßstab 1:3 angelegte Fußballfeld ein, welches das Herz des NikePark bildet. Hier haben Jugendliche die Gelegenheit, aus erster Hand zu erfahren, was es bedeutet, glanzvollen Fußball zu spielen.

Die Prinzipien französischer Parks: Schaffe eine Eingangssituation. Balance, Farben, Symmetrie. Schaffe einen abgegrenzten Raum. Schaffe Spaßbauten, Statuen.

Der Park ist innerhalb der Abfolge historischer Orte strategisch platziert, beginnend mit der Grande Arche hin zum Arc de Triomphe und weiter zu den Champs Elysees. Der Park wird so zu einem Teil der Pariser Stadtlandschaft. Die Besucher begreifen im NikePark die Verpflichtung von Nike, ultimativer Fußballausrüster zu sein: das Bestreben der Marke, Sportkleidung, Schuhe, weiteres Zubehör für den Bedarf von Spitzenathleten, aber auch für alle anderen zu schaffen, für Männer, Frauen und Kinder, die Fußball spielen und lieben. Und am wichtigsten wird sein, dass jeder am Ende diese Volksrepublik des Fußballs verlässt mit dem glücklichen Gefühl, einen Ort erlebt zu haben, wo sein Sport nicht begraben wird unter Strategie und Taktik, sondern immer noch Tempo hat und Spaß macht.

Nike Brand Design

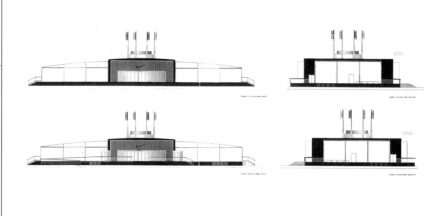

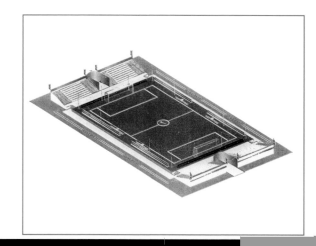

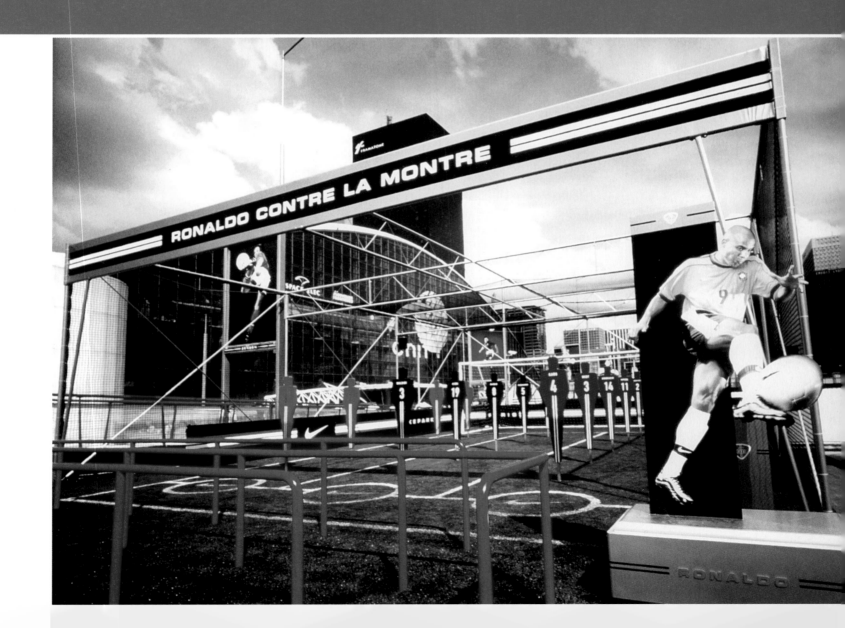

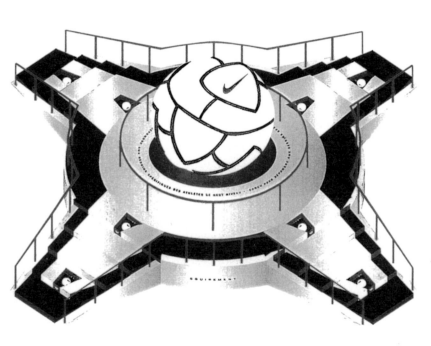

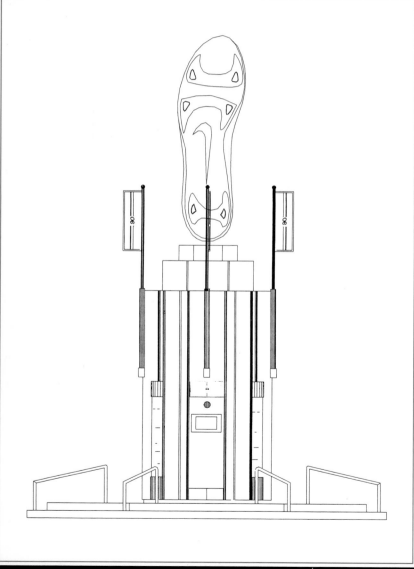

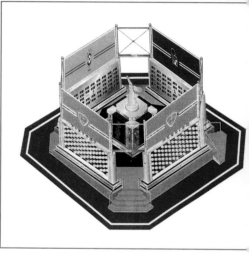

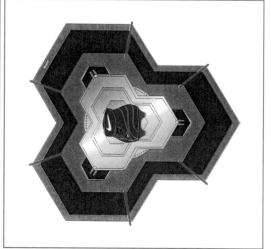

NikePark in front of Grande Arche (top); Drawing football shoe monument (bottom)
NikePark vor der Grande Arche (top); Zeichnung Fußball-Schuh-Monument (top)

Football shoe monument (top left); Drawing and floor plan pavilion (top right, bottom)

Pavilion interior and exterior (top)
Innen- und Außenansicht Pavillon (oben)

Fountain and championship locations billboard
Springbrunnen und Tafel mit Veranstaltungsorten Weltmeisterschaft

NikeTown, London

Project | Projekt: NikeTown London, Oxford Circus, 1999
Client | Bauherr: Nike Retail
Interior design | Innenarchitektur: BDP Design; Nike Retail Design
Project architects | Projektarchitekten: Nick Terry, Martin Cook, Stephen Anderson, Jack Hobbs,
          Sarah Turnbill, Rachel Brown, Grego Holm
Audiovisual consultants | AV-Planung: Electrosonic

NikeTown London – Oxford Circus

More than a store, NikeTown London is a place to come for inspiration, information, opportunities to play, first-class service and the very best sports products. NikeTown London at Oxford Circus is only the second NikeTown outside the US besides Berlin. At 6500 square metres it is the biggest NikeTown in the world, designed as a flagship store to rival New York's. It is the only place in UK where you will find the full range of Nike footwear, apparel and equipment. A place that many world-class athletes make their home, London was chosen as the destination for the 14th NikeTown because of its enormous energy, its cultural diversity and love of sports.

The joy of play

Encouraging and inspiring people to play sport is part of NikeTown's role in London. Visitors to the store can find out where to play sport in their area, join the NikeTown running club, attend a sports clinic, meet athletes and see powerful images of people playing and enjoying sport.

NikeTown staff in each specific pavilion are knowledgeable about their particular sport and can advise on the products that best suit customers' specific needs, as well as provide information on sports clubs and events in the capital.

Town within a town

NikeTown London spreads over three floors and is made up of separate 'buildings', each housing areas (sports 'pavilions') devoted to a specific sport. No two pavilions are the same and each has displays, products, interactives and staff concerned exclusively with that sport. There are pavilions for football, rugby, tennis, training, running, basketball, golf and ACG (All Conditions Gear) pavilions. The women's pavilion (housing all the women's sports products) takes most of the second floor and is the largest women's sports retail area in Europe.

NikeTown London – Oxford Circus

NikeTown London ist mehr als eine Verkaufsfläche. Hierher kommt man auf der Suche nach Anregungen, Informationen, Spielmöglichkeiten, Topservice und erstklassigen Sportprodukten. NikeTown London am Oxford Circus ist, neben Berlin, erst das zweite Projekt außerhalb der USA. Mit über 6.500 Quadratmetern ist es zugleich die größte NikeTown und steht als Flagshipstore im Wettbewerb mit New York.

Es ist der einzige Ort in Großbritannien, wo man die komplette Kollektion von Nike-Schuhen, -Kleidung und -Ausrüstung findet. Auf London fiel die Wahl als Standort der 14. NikeTown, weil hier viele Weltklassesportler zu Hause sind und die Stadt für enorme Energien, kulturelle Vielfalt und Sportbegeisterung steht.

Vergnügen am Spiel

Lust zu machen auf Sport ist Teil der Rolle von NikeTown in London. Besucher können sich darüber informieren, wo in ihrer Gegend sie Sport treiben können. Sie sind eingeladen, Mitglied im NikeTown Running Club zu werden. Sie können eine Sportklinik erleben, Athleten treffen und eindrucksvolle Bilder von Menschen beim Sport betrachten.

Das NikeTown-Team in jedem der einer Sportdisziplin gewidmeten Pavillons weiß nicht nur alles über die spezifische Gattung, es berät nicht nur über Produkte, die den Kundenbedürfnissen am besten entsprechen, es kann auch Auskünfte geben über Sportvereine und Sportereignisse in London.

Stadt in der Stadt

NikeTown London erstreckt sich über drei Geschosse und besteht aus verschiedenen 'Gebäuden', die als Pavillons jeweils eine einzelne Sportgattung repräsentieren. Keiner dieser Pavillons gleicht einem anderen, jeder verfügt über Ausstellungsobjekte, Produke, interaktive Angebote und Fachverkäufer, die sich ausschließlich dieser Disziplin widmen. Themen der Pavillons sind Fußball, Rugby, Tennis, Training,

The store also has its own 'Town Square' – the central point of activities and a stage for events like sports clinics, Q&A sessions with athletes, new product launches and a venue for the NikeTown London Running Club to meet for a pre-run stretch and warm-up. And just like any town, NikeTown London has its own streets, town plans and street signs.

The core

At the heart of the store lies the 'core'. It represents the one thing that lies at the heart of why people play sport – the sheer love of it. The core captures and brings to life the joy of play and connects Nike's passion for sport with its dedication to creating innovative and cutting-edge products.

A 3-storey, 360° multimedia projection screen encases a centrepiece called the 'chandelier'; a display of 750 photos that convey the joy of playing sport around the world, from professional to playground level. The photography is the work of the internationally acclaimed American reportage photographer Peter Turnley, with contributions from LA-based Tami Kennedy.

Visitors can walk up into the core to get a closer look at the chandelier, and to try the interactive displays that reveal the science and inspiration behind some of Nike's greatest products that surround it. These include a 'Frankenstein's shoe' display of the many different elements behind Nike's Mercurial football boot, and a mannequin explaining the science behind Nike's Dri-F.I.T fabric.

Every 20 minutes, the window shutters will close and the core will come to life. The screens become a canvas for showing inspirational footage of London at play; shot in London in the summer of 1998 exclusively for NikeTown London.

Inspired by London, designed for Londoners

The NikeTown designers – led by Creative Brand Director John Hoke – designed NikeTown to reflect London's sports heritage, its architecture and diversity. Just as

Laufen, Basketball, Golf und Allwetterausrüstung (All Conditions Gear – ACG). Der Pavillon für Sportlerinnen, wo alle Sportprodukte für Frauen gezeigt werden, nimmt den größten Teil des zweiten Obergeschosses ein und ist die größte Einzelhandelsfläche für weibliche Sportausrüstung in Europa.

NikeTown hat auch einen eigenen zentralen ‚Stadtplatz', der Mittelpunkt für Aktivitäten und Bühne für sportmedizinische Veranstaltungen, Interviewrunden mit Sportstars und neue Produktvorstellungen ist, außerdem Treffpunkt für den Nike-Town London Running Club als Lockerungs- und Warm-up-Bereich. Und wie jede Stadt ist NikeTown ausgestattet mit eigenen Straßen, Stadtplänen und Straßenschildern.

Das Herzstück

Zentrum von NikeTown London bildet das ‚Herzstück'. Es ist Ausdruck der eigentlichen Motivation, die Menschen zum Sport treibt – reine Freude und Hingabe. Das Herzstück lässt den Spaß am Spiel lebendig werden und verbindet Nikes Leidenschaft für den Sport mit der Verpflichtung, innovative und bahnbrechende Produkte zu schaffen.

Ein drei Geschosse hoher, 360-Grad Multimedia-Bildschirm umschließt eine zentrale Installation, den so genannten ‚Kronleuchter', dieser trägt 750 Fotos, die den Spaß am Sport rund um die Welt versinnbildlichen, vom Profibereich bis zum Kinderspielplatz. Die Fotos sind Werke des international bekannten amerikanischen Reportagefotografen Peter Turnley, ergänzt um einige Motive von Tami Kennedy aus Los Angeles. Besucher können in das ‚Herzstück' hineinspazieren, um einen näheren Blick auf den Kronleuchter zu werfen oder die interaktiven Ausstellungselemente zu nutzen, die das Know-how und die Inspiration enthüllen, wie sie in einigen der hier ebenfalls gezeigten besten Nike-Produkte stecken. Darunter sind ein ‚Frankenstein'-Schuhobjekt, das die verschiedenen Bestandteile von Nikes Mercurial Fußballschuh erklärt, und ein Mannequin, welches die wissenschaftlichen Grundlagen von Nikes Dri-F.I.T Textilstoff erläutert.

London has developed with old and new buildings side by side, NikeTown's buildings incorporate radically different design styles, from the traditional red brick of the football pavilion to the futuristic glass bricks of the golf pavilion.

The space is designed to reflect the features the designers felt to be unique and characteristic of London. These include the bricked-up windows of the rugby, basketball and football pavilions – a reference to the 18th-century window tax, where Londoners bricked up their windows to avoid paying a levy for each window overlooking the street. The store even has its own custom-designed manhole covers.

Besides global stars such as Ronaldo, Tiger Woods and Marion Jones, local and British stars such as Kelly Holmes, Lawrence Dallaglio and Jamie Redknapp appear on in-store displays and graphics at NikeTown London. Londoner Ray Mouncey and the British Milers Club are featured in the running pavilion, while the likes of Arsenal's Thierry Henry and Leeds United's Rio Ferdinand are featured in the football pavilion. Not content with pictures of these athletes at their finest sporting moments – the kids pavilion also displays pictures of them as children!

Nike Brand Design

Alle zwanzig Minuten werden die Fensteröffnungen geschlossen und das Herzstück erwacht zum Leben. Der Bildschirm ist dann Leinwand für stimulierende Bilder von London beim Spiel, eingefangen exklusiv für NikeTown im Sommer 1998.

Inspiriert von London, gestaltet für London

Die Gestalter – unter der Leitung von Creative Brand Director John Hoke – entwarfen NikeTown London als Reflexion auf das sportliche Erbe, die Architektur und Vielfalt dieser Stadt. So wie London sich entwickelte als Einheit aus alten und neuen Gebäuden, vereint NikeTown radikal verschiedene Stile, vom traditionellen Backsteinmauerwerk des Fußball-Pavillons bis zum futuristischen Glasbaustein des Golf-Pavillons.

Der gesamte Raum wurde nach der Maßgabe gestaltet, die Merkmale wiederzugeben, die für London charakteristisch und einzigartig sind. Wie zum Beispiel die zugemauerten Fensteröffnungen der Rugby-, Basketball- und Fußball-Pavillons – eine Referenz an die ‚Fenstersteuer' des 18. Jahrhunderts, als die Londoner ihre Fenster vermauerten, um den Tribut für jedes einzelne straßenseitige Fenster zu vermeiden. NikeTown hat sogar eigene, maßgefertigte Kanaldeckel.

Neben Weltstars wie Ronaldo, Tiger Woods und Marion Jones werden auch regionale und britische Sportgrößen wie Kelly Holmes, Lawrence Dallaglio und Jamie Redknapp in NikeTown prominent im Bild und mit Erinnerungsstücken vorgestellt. Der Londoner Ray Mouncey und der British Milers Club haben ihren Auftritt im Lauf-Pavillon, Arsenal's Thierry Henry und Leeds United's Rio Ferdinand im Fußball-Pavillon. Dabei bleibt es nicht bei Fotos ihrer größten sportlichen Momente, im Kinderpavillon kann man die gleichen Helden auch in ganz jungen Jahren bewundern.

Nike Brand Design

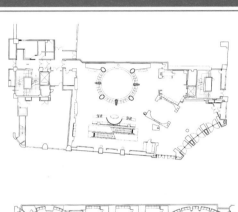

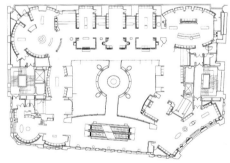

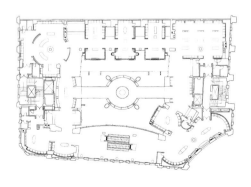

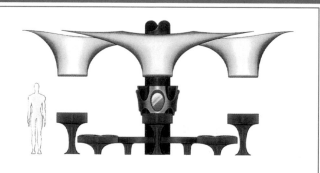

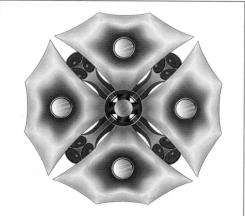

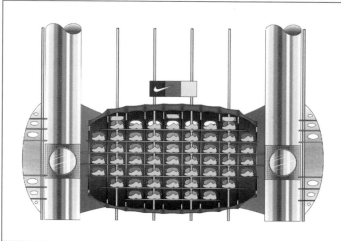

Display area footwear (top); drawings aerial view seating area (bottom)
Präsentationsbereich Sportschuhe (oben); Zeichnungen Vogelperspektive Sitzbereich (unten)

Details seating area (top) and display system footwear (bottom)

Display and seating area footwear
Präsentations- und Anprobebereich Sportschuhe

Display system footwear
Regalsystem Sportschuhe

BMW: Event and Delivery Center, Munich
Erlebnis- und Auslieferungszentrum, München

Competition | Wettbewerb 2001

Vision

The BMW Group is planning to build a centre for brand experience and vehicle delivery (working title: BMW Event and Delivery Center). Customers from all over the world will be invited to take possession of their new BMW automobile personally and enjoy an unforgettable live experience of the BMW brand in an atmosphere of exclusivity. Over and above that, the BMW Event and Delivery Center's foremost objective is to create a sustained emotional bond between the BMW world and the general public. The number of visitors is expected to be several hundred thousands per year. The BMW Event and Delivery Center, in spatial and spiritual unity with the world-famous BMW Tower – the Group's headquarters – and the BMW Museum, will become the architectural showcase of the BMW brand. The Center is meant not only to reflect BMW's corporate identity, but also to give it a shape that will last.

Core values of the Event and Delivery Center

On the basis of the values currently symbolized by the BMW brand – dynamism, challenge and culture – new core values have been defined for the BMW Event and Delivery Center. These are "persuasive power", "motion" and "individuality". As before, the focus is on the key emotion of "joy". Thus, a different objective is assigned to each of the four areas of the Center: to deepen joy, to multiply joy, to arouse joy and to propagate joy. This matrix of values and thematic foci forms the basis of the BMW Event and Delivery Center's identity.

Site

The Event and Delivery Center's site is unique and of immense public importance. For one thing, the Center will be located in the immediate vicinity of the Group's headquarters, the BMW Museum and the original BMW factory, and for another, it will border on the Olympic Park, year in year out the destination of numerous visitors. This close contact between BMW and the general public creates a huge functional and spiritual potential that should be exploited. Located in the exciting neighbourhood of the existing world-famous ensemble, the Event and Delivery Center will be another landmark – a new symbol not only of the BMW Group, but also of the city of Munich.

Vision

Die BMW Group hat beschlossen, ein Zentrum für Markenerlebnis- und Fahrzeugauslieferung zu schaffen (Arbeitstitel: BMW Erlebnis- und Auslieferungszentrum). Kunden aus aller Welt werden eingeladen sein, ihr neues BMW-Automobil persönlich abzuholen und in einer Aura der Exklusivität eine unvergessliche Live-Erfahrung mit der Marke BMW zu erleben. Darüber hinaus hat das BMW Erlebnis- und Auslieferungszentrum das übergeordnete Ziel, eine langfristige emotionale Verankerung zwischen der Welt von BMW und der Öffentlichkeit zu schaffen; es werden mehrere Hunderttausend Besucher pro Jahr erwartet.

In räumlicher und ideeller Einheit mit dem schon heute weltweit bekannten Hochhaus – dem Sitz der Konzernzentrale – und dem BMW-Museum wird das BMW Erlebnis- und Auslieferungszentrum zum wegweisenden architektonischen Herzstück der Marke BMW werden: Es soll die BMW-Identität nicht nur widerspiegeln, sondern nachhaltig prägen.

Kernwerte des Erlebnis- und Auslieferungszentrums

Ausgehend von den bestehenden Werten der Marke BMW – dynamisch, herausfordernd, kultiviert – wurden für das BMW Erlebnis- und Auslieferungszentrum eigene Kernwerte definiert. Sie lauten: „überzeugend", „bewegend", und „individuell". Im Zentrum steht dabei nach wie vor die Schlüssel-Emotion „Freude". Für jeden der vier Bereiche des Zentrums ergibt sich somit eine andere Aufgabe: Freude vertiefen, Freude vervielfachen, Freude entfachen und Freude verbreiten. Diese Matrix aus Werten und thematischen Schwerpunkten bildet die Grundlage für die Identität des BMW Erlebnis- und Auslieferungszentrums.

Standort

Der Standort des Erlebnis- und Auslieferungszentrums ist einzigartig und von großer öffentlicher Bedeutung. Es steht in unmittelbarer Nähe zur Konzernzentrale, dem BMW-Museum und dem BMW-Stammwerk einerseits und zum Olympiapark mit seinem hohen Publikumsaufkommen andererseits. Durch diese Verbindung zwischen BMW und Öffentlichkeit entsteht ein großes funktionales wie ideelles Potenzial, das es auszuschöpfen gilt. In stimulierender Nähe zu den bereits weltbekannten Gebäu-

Concept

The Event and Delivery Center is intended to be perceived not just as the BMW Group's billboard. Rather, the project should form the actual focal point for the meeting of three different worlds that complement and significantly enhance each other.
– The world of the BMW brand and the BMW Group: The customers who personally come to the Event and Delivery Center to take possession of their new automobiles completely immerse themselves in this world. The sustained memory of this experience creates a lasting emotional bond with the BMW brand.
– The world of manufacturing: The manufacture of a car is a process of substantial fascinating power. Especially in today's services-oriented society, a visit to a factory where, despite all its high-tech automation, manual skills are still as indispensable as they were in the past, is an extraordinary experience.
– The world of leisure in the tourist centre of Munich: The great variety of recreational facilities and the distinctive charm of Bavaria's capital enjoy an excellent reputation both at home and abroad. A visit to the Event and Delivery Center will always be a visit to the city of Munich as well.

Target groups

The BMW Event and Delivery Center will address four different target groups, all of whom are equally invited to immerse themselves in the BMW world and gain an authentic experience of its technology, products and fascinating atmosphere.
– The primary target group are those BMW clients who want to take possession of their new car directly at its "place of birth". On this occasion, the BMW Group, its products and manufacturing processes will be presented to them in a manner that creates a lasting impression in a hitherto unknown dimension.
– For the visitors to the Olympic Park – approximately 6 million per year – as well as for visitors to the city of Munich in general, the BMW Event and Delivery Center will be an additional exciting centre of attraction. The BMW Group, as a player on the world stage, will extend a heartfelt welcome to them.
– The third target group is the BMW brand's friends and fans who, keenly interested in the company's development and its ramifications, its products and manufacturing processes, desire a personal experience of all these facets.

den soll mit dem Erlebnis- und Auslieferungszentrum ein weiteres Wahrzeichen entstehen – nicht nur für die BMW Group, sondern auch für die Stadt München.

Konzept

Das Erlebnis- und Auslieferungszentrum soll nicht alleine als Aushängeschild der BMW Group wahrgenommen werden. Das Projekt muss vielmehr einen eigenen Kristallisationspunkt von drei verschiedenen Welten darstellen, die sich gegenseitig ergänzen und potenzieren.
– Die Welt der Marke BMW und der BMW Group: Wer sein neues Automobil persönlich im Erlebnis- und Auslieferungszentrum abholt, taucht vollständig in diese Welt ein. Dieses nachhaltige Erlebnis schafft eine dauerhafte, emotionale Bindung zur Marke BMW.
– Die Welt der Produktion: Die Fertigung eines Automobils ist ein Prozess, von dem eine große Faszination ausgeht. Gerade in der heutigen Dienstleistungsgesellschaft ist der Besuch eines Werkes, in dem bei aller High-Tech auch handwerkliches Können und Geschick noch immer unverzichtbar sind, ein außergewöhnliches Ereignis.
– Die Freizeitwelt der Tourismusmetropole München: Die Vielfalt des Angebots und der ganz besondere Charme der bayerischen Landeshauptstadt genießen weit über die Landesgrenzen hinaus einen ausgezeichneten Ruf. Der Besuch im Erlebnis- und Auslieferungszentrum ist immer auch ein Besuch der Stadt München.

Zielgruppen

Das BMW Erlebnis- und Auslieferungszentrum richtet sich an vier Zielgruppen. Alle sind gleichermaßen eingeladen, in die BMW-Welt einzutauchen und eine authentische Erfahrung mit der Technik, den Produkten und der Faszination dieser Welt zu machen.
– Primäre Zielgruppe sind die Kunden, die ihr Fahrzeug direkt am „Geburtsort" abholen möchten. Ihnen werden bei dieser Gelegenheit die BMW Group sowie deren Produkte und Produktionsprozesse als nachhaltiges Erlebnis in einer neuen Dimension präsentiert.
– Eine weitere Zielgruppe sind die jährlich ca. 10 Mio. Besucher des Olympiaparks sowie die Besucher der Landeshauptstadt München. Für sie wird das BMW Erlebnis-

– Finally, BMW employees, journalists, car dealers, visitors and the natives of Munich will use the BMW Event and Delivery Center as a new meeting place and a venue with a unique programme of events.

Design objective

This competition is intended to produce an architectural structure of distinctive design and outstanding operational qualities that at the same time symbolizes the world of the BMW brand. The competition's central task is to devise a solution that assures the harmonious integration of the new building and its open-air facilities into the context of the distinctive, high-quality structures of the Olympic Park and the present BMW complex.

The Event and Delivery Center will give both the BMW Group and the city of Munich the opportunity to add another jewel to the existing architectural crown, and to encance this unique site even further.

Experience of the brand

Customers and visitors encounter the BMW brand in various situations and media. For the brand to be perceived as unique and outstanding, each of these encounters must purposefully be transformed into a fascinating experience.

Taken together, these form a chain of experiences that spans all the way from the first promise via various confirmations to the final fulfilment of the promise by the product. Within this chain, architecture constitutes an element that is able to arouse and support expectations.

The degree of esteem that each client or visitor feels for the building and the experience it offers is of outstanding importance as it transforms these emotions into envoys of the company.

Event and Delivery Center

Obviously, the premium positioning of the BMW brand is also valid for the Event and Delivery Center. For this, BMW's existing core values – dynamism, challenge and culture – were translated as "persuasive power", "motion" and "individuality", the focus being, as before, on the key emotion of "joy".

und Auslieferungszentrum einen weiteren faszinierenden Anziehungspunkt darstellen.

– Dritte Zielgruppe sind Freunde und Bewunderer der Marke BMW, die an der Entwicklung der Firma und ihrem Umfeld, an den Produkten und den Produktionsprozessen regen Anteil nehmen und all diese Aspekte persönlich erleben wollen.

– Schließlich gewinnen BMW-Mitarbeiter, Pressevertreter, Händler, Gäste und Bewohner der Stadt München mit dem BMW Erlebnis- und Auslieferungszentrum einen neuen Treffpunkt und Veranstaltungsort mit einem einzigartigen Programm.

Entwurfsziel

Dieser Wettbewerb soll ein Bauwerk von herausragender und charakteristischer Architektur, Gestaltung und Organisation hervorbringen, das zugleich die Welt der Marke BMW repräsentiert. Zentrale Aufgabe ist es, das neue Gebäude und seine Außenanlagen in respektvoller Harmonie in den Kontext der charakterstarken und hochwertigen Gebäude des Olympiaparks und der BMW Group einzubinden. Mit dem Erlebnis- und Auslieferungszentrum bietet sich der BMW Group sowie der Stadt München die Chance, das bestehende bedeutende Gebäude-Ensemble und den Landschaftsraum um ein weiteres Juwel zu ergänzen und den Standort in seiner Einzigartigkeit zu profilieren.

Markenerlebnis

Die Kunden und Besucher begegnen der Marke BMW in verschiedenen Situationen und Medien. Damit die Marke insgesamt als einzigartig und hervorragend wahrgenommen wird, muss jede dieser Begegnungen gezielt zu einem faszinierenden Erlebnis gemacht werden. Zusammen bilden die Erlebnisse eine so genannte Erlebniskette, die vom ersten Versprechen über vielfältige Bestätigungen bis hin zur Erfüllung des Versprechens durch das Produkt reicht. Die Architektur stellt in dieser Kette einen Faktor dar, der Erwartungen erwecken und unterstützen kann. Die persönliche Wertschätzung der Kunden und Besucher für das Gebäude und seine Erlebnisangebote ist von herausragender Bedeutung, da es diese zu Botschaftern des Unternehmens werden lässt.

For the BMW Group, the Event and Delivery Center forms a pivotal element in how the company presents itself to the general public, and in its novel organization of vehicle delivery. The BMW Group intends to present itself as innovative, commanding, compact, cosmopolitan and authentic, without having to resort to fake elements of entertainment. The Event and Delivery Center is the place where the BMW Group exposes its philosophy and the guidelines of its actions, and presents its employees and products to the general public. The values they represent determine the character of the Event and Delivery Center.

The building's architecture, its interior and exterior spaces, must live up to these demanding aspirations with regard to design quality and functionality. The brief is to design an outstanding individual object, whose own identity and quality, right down to the smallest detail, reflects the BMW Group's philosophy and forms a harmonious whole with the surrounding buildings, green areas, open-air spaces and traffic facilities. The conditions imposed with regard to the protection of historic monuments must be respected.

The Event and Delivery Center possesses a clear premium character. An atmosphere of exclusivity and high class can be felt at any time and in each single one of its spaces. Thus, the task consists in creating, from space to space and from platform to platform, a consistent chain of experiences. The BMW Event and Delivery Center is divided into four areas that intersect each other spatially and thematically: BMW World, the Hall, BMW Premiere and the Forum. A succinct description of each of these is given below.

BMW World

BMW World represents all the facets of the BMW brand. It is unique, fascinating and overwhelming at first glance. In the BMW World, the whole gamut of BMW products and services is displayed and emotionally conveyed to the visitor. Each of BMW's activities and departments is here given a platform to present itself and to integrate into a greater whole. One cannot withdraw oneself from the BMW World. It is the all-pervading pivotal element of the BMW Event and Delivery Center. One will always return to this world. To symbolize this experience, the reception desk is not located at the entrance, but in the centre of this area.

Erlebnis- und Auslieferungszentrum

Die Premium-Positionierung der Marke BMW gilt selbstverständlich auch für das Erlebnis- und Auslieferungszentrum. Die bestehenden Kernwerte von BMW – dynamisch, herausfordernd, kultiviert – wurden für das EAZ übersetzt. Sie lauten: „überzeugend", „bewegend" und „individuell". Im Zentrum steht dabei nach wie vor die Schlüssel-Emotion „Freude". Das Erlebnis- und Auslieferungszentrum bildet für die BMW Group einen zentralen Baustein in der Präsentation des Unternehmens in der Öffentlichkeit und in der Neuorganisation der Fahrzeugauslieferung. Die BMW Group will sich im Erlebnis- und Auslieferungszentrum innovativ, souverän, kompakt, weltoffen und authentisch präsentieren ohne aufgesetzte Unterhaltungselemente hinzufügen zu müssen. Es ist der Ort, an dem die BMW Group ihre Philosophie und die Leitlinien ihres Handelns sowie ihre Mitarbeiter und Produkte der Öffentlichkeit darstellt. Die darin niedergelegten Werte bestimmen die Welt des Erlebnis- und Auslieferungszentrums.

Diesen hohen gestalterischen und funktionalen Ansprüchen müssen die Architektur des Gebäudes, seine Innen- und Außenräume entsprechen. Es wird der Entwurf eines herausragenden Einzelobjekts erwartet, dessen eigene Identität und Qualität bis ins Detail der Philosophie der BMW Group entspricht und mit den umliegenden Gebäuden, Grün-, Frei- und Verkehrsräumen ein harmonisches Ensemble bildet. Die Belange des Denkmalschutzes sind zu beachten. Das BMW Erlebnis- und Auslieferungszentrum hat einen klaren Premium-Charakter. Die Atmosphäre von Exklusivität und Klasse ist jederzeit spürbar, in jedem einzelnen Raum. Es gilt also, von Raum zu Raum bzw. von Plattform zu Plattform eine konsistente „Erlebniskette" zu schaffen. Das BMW Erlebnis- und Auslieferungszentrum ist in vier Bereiche aufgeteilt, die sich räumlich und inhaltlich überschneiden.

BMW Welt

Die BMW Welt stellt alle Facetten der Marke BMW dar. Sie ist einmalig, faszinierend und auf den ersten Blick überwältigend. In der BMW Welt wird der volle Umfang aller BMW-Produkte und -Leistungen gezeigt und erlebbar gemacht. Jede Aktivität, jeder Bereich von BMW erhält hier eine Plattform, um sich zu präsentieren und Teil eines größeren Ganzen zu werden. Der BMW Welt kann man sich nicht entziehen; sie ist

Hall

The Hall is the Event and Delivery Center's public space. Shops and boutiques, restaurants and cafés, child-care facilities and the promenade are located here. For the general public, the Hall serves the same function that the BMW World serves for the BMW brand: like a portal, it provides initial access to the BMW Event and Delivery Center. The BMW World and the Hall are not separated from each other. Both spatially and spiritually, their areas merge into each other, create interaction and thus form a field of tension between the BMW brand and the general public. In this field of tension is the very essence of the BMW Event and Delivery Center: "encounter".

BMW Premiere

As soon as an atmosphere of encounter has been created in the field of tension between BMW and the general public, the actual core of the BMW Event and Delivery Center comes into the focus of attention: the Premiere. The BMW Premiere is the vehicle delivery section of the BMW Event and Delivery Center. All visitors can observe it, but it is not accessible for all: access is restricted to customers collecting their new vehicle, accompanying persons and BMW's special guests. This also serves to create an aura of exclusivity that arouses desire. BMW Premiere is the innermost sanctum of the BMW Event and Delivery Center. The handing-over of the vehicle forms the dramatic climax of the visit. It is carried out in a perfectly staged high-tech environment. At every moment of this unforgettable, authentic experience of the BMW brand, the culture of dynamics, motion and joy can be felt. All other areas of the BMW Event and Delivery Center are stages or spatial platforms for BMW Premiere, all of highest quality and finely tuned to each other.

der allgegenwärtige Dreh- und Angelpunkt des BMW Erlebnis- und Auslieferungszentrums. Zu ihr kehrt man immer wieder zurück. Sinngemäß steht auch der Empfangscounter nicht am Eingang, sondern in der Mitte dieses Bereiches.

Hall

Die Hall ist der öffentliche Bereich des BMW Erlebnis- und Auslieferungszentrums. Hier befinden sich Shops und Boutiquen, Restaurants und Cafés, Kinderbetreuung und die Promenade. Die Hall erfüllt für die Öffentlichkeit beziehungsweise das Publikum die gleiche Funktion wie die BMW Welt für die Marke BMW: Sie stellt, einem Portal gleich, den ersten Zugang zum BMW Erlebnis- und Auslieferungszentrum her. BMW Welt und Hall sind nicht voneinander getrennt. Sowohl räumlich als auch ideell gehen die beiden Bereiche ineinander über, schaffen Interaktion und bilden so ein Spannungsfeld zwischen der Marke BMW und der Öffentlichkeit. In diesem Spannungsfeld entsteht, was das Wesen des BMW Erlebnis- und Auslieferungszentrums ausmacht: „Begegnung".

BMW Premiere

So wie im Spannungsfeld zwischen BMW und Öffentlichkeit die Atmosphäre der Begegnung geschaffen ist, rückt der eigentliche Kern des BMW Erlebnis- und Auslieferungszentrums ins Zentrum der Aufmerksamkeit: die Premiere. Die BMW Premiere ist die Fahrzeugauslieferung des BMW Erlebnis- und Auslieferungszentrums. Sie ist für alle Besucher einsehbar, aber nicht für alle zugänglich: Sie bleibt den Abholern, deren Begleitung und besonderen Gästen des Hauses BMW vorbehalten. Auch dadurch wird eine Aura des Besonderen und Exklusiven geschaffen, die ein Begehren weckt. Die BMW Premiere ist das innere Sanktum des gesamten Ortes BMW Erlebnis- und Auslieferungszentrum. Die Fahrzeugübergabe bildet den dramaturgischen Höhepunkt des Besuchs. Sie findet in einem perfekt inszenierten High-Tech-Umfeld statt.

Zu jedem Zeitpunkt dieses unvergesslichen, authentischen Ereignisses mit der Marke BMW ist die Kultur der Dynamik, Bewegung und Freude spürbar. Alle anderen Bereiche des BMW Erlebnis- und Auslieferungszentrums stellen für die BMW

######## Forum

The Forum is the venue for internal and public events. It provides a hall with a large-scale screen and different possibilities for seating (300 seats for parliament-style seating, 600 seats for movie audiences). As a special feature, the Forum is open not just when events are held. Rather, it forms an integral part of the BMW Event and Delivery Center, being open toward the Hall all day long, while its large-scale screen continuously shows pictures from the fascinating world of automobiles and BMW. The Forum contributes to the overall atmospheric impression of the BMW Event and Delivery Center.

######## Summary

All four areas fit together to form a harmonious whole that has been carefully thought out right to the smallest detail. The relaxed and lavish atmosphere is imbued with candour and hospitality and impinges on all senses equally, thus giving rise to a symbiosis of warm-heartedness and high tech, of tradition and innovation.

The BMW Event and Delivery Center gives all visitors a fascinating, unforgettable experience of the BMW brand's world. At the core of this experience is the same key emotion that is also of central importance for the BMW brand: joy. Altogether, the Event and Delivery Center's four areas and their functions within the general concept can be summed up as four different shades of the key emotion of joy.

– The BMW World is intended to deepen joy.
– The Hall is intended to multiply joy.
– The Premiere is intended to arouse joy.
– The Forum is intended to propagate joy.

BMW AG

Premiere eine dramaturgische und räumliche Plattform dar, hochwertig und bis ins kleinste Detail aufeinander abgestimmt.

######## Forum

Das Forum ist der Ort für interne und externe Veranstaltungen. Es bietet einen Veranstaltungssaal mit Großleinwand und verschiedenen Möglichkeiten der Bestuhlung (300 Sitzplätze bei parlamentarischer Bestuhlung, 600 Sitzplätze bei Kinobestuhlung). Als Besonderheit ist das Forum nicht nur bei Veranstaltungen geöffnet. Es bildet vielmehr einen integralen Bestandteil des BMW Erlebnis- und Auslieferungszentrums: Es steht auch im täglichen Betrieb zur Hall hin offen, wobei auf einer Großleinwand laufend Bilder aus der faszinierenden Welt des Automobils und BMW zu sehen sind. Das Forum leistet einen Beitrag zum atmosphärischen Gesamteindruck des BMW Erlebnis- und Auslieferungszentrums.

######## Zusammenfassung

Alle vier Bereiche fügen sich zu einem harmonischen und bis ins Detail durchdachten Ganzen zusammen. Die entspannte und großzügige Atmosphäre ist durchdrungen von Offenheit und Gastfreundschaft und spricht alle Sinne gleichermaßen an. So entsteht eine Symbiose von Herzlichkeit und High-Tech, von Tradition und Innovation. Das BMW Erlebnis- und Auslieferungszentrum bietet allen Besuchern ein faszinierendes, unvergessliches Erlebnis mit der Welt der Marke BMW. Im Kern dieses Erlebnisses steht dieselbe Schlüssel-Emotion, welche auch für die Marke BMW von zentraler Bedeutung ist: Freude. Rückblickend können die vier Bereiche und ihre Funktionen innerhalb des Gesamtkonzeptes noch einmal als verschiedene Schattierungen der Schlüssel-Emotion Freude dargestellt werden.

– Die BMW Welt soll Freude vertiefen.
– Die Hall soll Freude vervielfachen.
– Die Premiere soll Freude entfachen.
– Das Forum soll Freude verbreiten.

BMW AG

"Clean Energy Cloud"

The cloud is largely free of functional spaces: the aim was to create a light, ecological and technically optimized transparent construction – a "Clean Energy Cloud" that controls the various building management functions (natural and mechanical ventilation, air conditioning, energy production, and the variable lighting system based on fibre-optic light tubes and roller blinds). Only the lounge areas are located – like the capsules of a zeppelin – inside the cloud construction. These areas were designed over two and a half storeys so as to offer views of the BMW Tower and the Premiere, and insight into the construction.

The shape of the cloud was created in response to the functions below it (attract and repulse), the main views from the building (of the tower and museum) and technical/constructional requirements (natural air circulation, smoke extraction). By relocating the vehicle delivery area and the forum outside the cloud, the overall height of the building was reduced by around 6 metres, bringing it to the same level as the BMW Museum. Nonetheless, the building still features floor-to-ceiling heights of between 8 and 20 metres. The cloud is supported by a structure running all the way round the building, set 5 metres within its outer edge, creating a large, pillar-free space. The water that drains from the large roof surface is collected in a tank and can be used for industrial purposes.

Premiere

Premiere, the vehicle delivery facility, was built on slightly raised ground close to street level. The lounges above it are accessed by escalator through a wedge-shaped opening cut into the cloud – providing a view of the BMW Tower from the park side entrance. Exhaust fumes are extracted through a sub-floor. In this area the cloud is fitted with mobile smoke extraction panels, which emerge from the soffit if a fire is detected.

„Clean Energy Cloud"

Die Wolke wurde größtenteils von Funktionsflächen entlastet, zugunsten einer leichten, ökologisch und gebäudetechnisch optimierten, transparenten Konstruktion, und wird dadurch zur „Clean Energy Cloud", welche die Funktionen der natürlichen beziehungsweise mechanischen Belüftung, der Kühlung, der Energiegewinnung und der geregelten und inszenierbaren Belichtung mittels Lichtpipes und Sonnenschutzrollos regelt. Lediglich die Bereiche der Lounges befinden sich wie die Kapsel eines Zeppelins innerhalb der Konstruktion der Wolke. Diese Bereiche wurden in Hinblick auf Aussicht sowohl auf das BMW-Hochhaus als auch auf die Premiere und auf Einblicke in die Konstruktion auf zweieinhalb Geschossen konzipiert.

Die Form der Wolke wurde in Bezug zu den darunterliegenden Funktionen (Anziehen und Abstoßen), den wichtigen Ausblicken aus dem Gebäude (Sicht auf Hochhaus und Museum) und technisch-konstruktiven Erfordernissen (natürliche Luftzirkulation, Brandrauchentlüftung) generiert. Durch das Verlegen der Fahrzeugauslieferung und des Forums aus der Wolke wurde die Gebäudehöhe um cirka 6 Meter auf die Höhe des BMW-Museums abgesenkt. Es verbleiben nach wie vor lichte Raumhöhen zwischen 8 und 20 Meter. Aufgelagert wird die Wolke auf einem umlaufend 5 Meter hinter die Vorderkante versetzten Hauptkonstruktionsraster, wodurch ein großer stützenfreier Raum möglich wird. Die Abwässer der großen Dachfläche werden in einer Zisterne gesammelt und können als Brauchwasser verwendet werden.

Premiere

Die Auslieferung der Fahrzeuge, die Premiere, wurde auf einer leichten Erhöhung auf straßennahem Niveau realisiert. Die Erschließung der darüber liegenden Lounges erfolgt über Rolltreppen durch einen aus der Wolke ausgeschnittenen Sichtkeil, welcher bereits vom parkseitigen Eingang die Sicht auf das BMW-Hochhaus freigibt. Die Absaugung der Abgase erfolgt über einen Unterboden. In diesem Bereich werden in

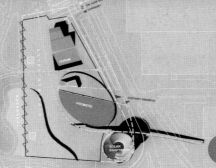

Forum

The forum consists of a sunken central area, which is modular and flexible, and a fixed platform providing nearly as much capacity as the required extensions. This minimizes the conversion work required for major events, while the remaining area can be used flexibly, like a large hall. The flexibility is created by a false floor, which contains all the various building services equipment: ventilation, air conditioning, power supply and sprinkler lines. As a result, all the exhibition and retail areas can be designed as "buildings within a building".

Double cone

The double cone at the southern entrance fulfils a number of functions: as an exhibition space and a communications area opening onto the street, as an entrance both to the main hall and to the group centre, and as a solar power plant. Its upper segment acts as a PV heliostat system, which provides energy for hydrogen production. The heliostats – mobile, and automatically turned towards the sun – are located on the interior of the cone and reflect the sun's rays onto a receiver, generating both electric power and thermal energy. The spiral ramp around the double cone provides access both to the connecting bridge and to the press café, as well as offering views into the solar power plant. The group centre is on the lower ground floor (level 1), connecting directly with the car park level and the main hall.

Coop Himmelblau

der Wolke mobile Rauchschürzen, welche im Brandfall aus der Untersicht ausgefahren werden, eingebaut.

Forum

Das Forum besteht aus einem abgesenkten Kernbereich, welcher flexibel bespiel- und teilbar ist und einer fixen Tribüne, welche annähernd die Kapazität der geforderten Erweiterungsflächen bietet. Somit sind bei Großveranstaltungen nur geringe Umbauarbeiten erforderlich und die restlichen Flächen im Sinne einer großen Halle flexibel nutzbar. Die Flexibilität wird durch einen Doppelboden gewährleistet, welcher Anlagen zur Be- und Entlüftung, Kühlung, Stromversorgung und Löschmittelleitungen enthält. Sämtliche Ausstellungs- und Shopbereiche können somit als Haus-im-Haus-System konzipiert werden.

Doppelkegel

Der Doppelkegel am südlichen Eingang ist mehrfach belegt: als Ausstellungsraum und Kommunikationselement zum Straßenraum, als Eingang sowohl in die Halle als auch in das Gruppenzentrum und als Solarkraftwerk. Im oberen Segment dient er als PV-Heliostatenanlage, welche Energie für die Wasserstoffgewinnung liefert. Die beweglichen und automatisch der Sonne nachgeführten Heliostaten sind an der Innenseite des Kegelmantels situiert und reflektieren die Sonnenstrahlen auf einen Receiver, wobei sowohl elektrischer Strom als auch thermische Energie gewonnen werden. Die Spiralrampe um den Doppelkegel ist einerseits Aufgang auf die Verbindungsbrücke, andererseits ein Zugang zum Pressecafé und ermöglicht Einblicke in das Solarkraftwerk. Im ersten Untergeschoss befindet sich das Gruppenzentrum, welches direkt an das Parkgeschoss und die große Halle angebunden ist.

Coop Himmelblau

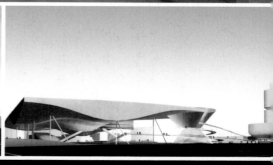

Model Clean Energy Cloud (top); interior view car presentation area (middle)
Modell Clean Energy Cloud (oben); Innenansicht Fahrzeughalle (Mitte)

Model views with existing BMW Museum and headquarters (bottom)
Modellansichten mit BMW Museum und Hochhaus (unten)

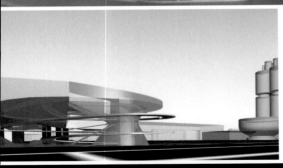

Model interior view car presentation area (top); ramp delivery area (middle)
Modellinnenansicht Fahrzeughalle (oben); Rampe Auslieferung (Mitte)

Drawings Event and Delivery Center (bottom)
Zeichnungen Erlebnis- und Auslieferungszentrum (unten)

The concept

The BMW Event and Delivery Center presents a generously proportioned architectural landscape integrated into the gentle slopes of the Olympic Park. The three focal areas – "event", "exhibition" and "performance" – are brought together under a bold, sweeping roof structure. The BMW Promenade, which runs from the Park, through the Center, and on to the BMW complex, forges a strong link between the Event and Delivery Center and the general public. The buildings are technically advanced, inspiring worlds of architecture, providing a generous and discreetly elegant stage for the products of the BMW brand.

Valleys and clouds

The building is designed to extend and echo the park landscape using architectural means. Its three primary components – "World", "Forum" and "Premiere" – are set in three artificial "valleys" with the large "Cloud" of the common roof structure floating above them. The space between the three valleys functions on two levels – as an access area, and as the main hub for all sections of the ensemble as a whole.

Sauerbruch Hutton Architekten

Gesamtkonzept

Das BMW Erlebnis- und Auslieferungszentrum (EAZ) besteht aus einer großzügigen, architektonischen Landschaft, die in die sanften Hügel des Olympiaparkes integriert ist. Die drei Brennpunkte „event", „exhibition" und „performance" sind unter einem kühnen, weitausgreifenden Dach zusammengefasst. Die BMW-Promenade, die den Park durch das Zentrum hindurch mit dem Stammgelände verbindet, bietet eine enge Beziehung und Verknüpfung des EAZ mit der Öffentlichkeit. Die Gebäude bilden technisch versierte, begeisternde architektonische Welten, die den Produkten der Marke BMW eine großzügige und unaufdringlich feine Bühne bieten.

Täler und Wolken

Das Gebäude ist als eine Fortsetzung der Parklandschaft mit architektonischen Mitteln konzipiert. Seine drei Hauptelemente „Welt", „Forum", und „Premiere" sind in drei künstlichen „Tälern" eingebettet, über denen die große "Wolke" eines durchgehenden Daches schwebt. Der Raum zwischen den drei „Tälern" fungiert auf zwei Ebenen als Erschließungsraum und Hauptverteiler für alle Teile des Gesamtensembles.

Sauerbruch Hutton Architekten

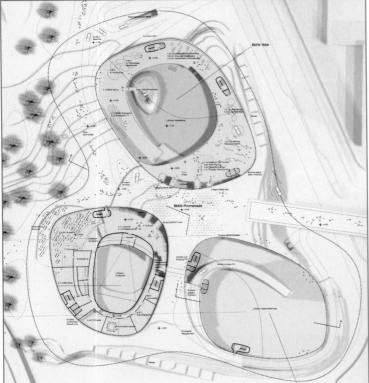

Model of Event and Delivery Center planned next to BMW headquarters (top); site plan (middle)

Modell Erlebnis- und Auslieferungszentrum mit bestehendem BMW-Hochhaus (oben); Lageplan (Mitte)

Model exterior view (bottom)

Modell Außenansicht (unten)

Drawings interior view car presentation area (top); exterior views (middle)
Zeichnungen Innenansicht Fahrzeughalle (oben); Außenansichten (Mitte)

Model exterior view and perspective of public hall (bottom)
Modell Außenansicht und Blick in Publikumsbereich (unten)

CAD exterior view with existing BMW tower (top); drawing roof construction (bottom)
CAD-Außenansicht mit bestehendem BMW-Hochhaus (oben); Zeichnung Dachkonstruktion (unten)

CAD exterior views (middle and bottom)
CAD-Außenansichten (Mitte und unten)

Atmosphere and aesthetic mission

The BMW Event and Delivery Center is designed to stage the handover of the new vehicle to the customer as an unforgettable event. The premium positioning of the BMW brand implies a high level of expectation – and the Center has to fulfil these expectations. To fascinate visitors requires more than just high-quality functionalism – it calls for an astounding sequence of spatial experiences, creating a theatre for the dramatization of customer service. To trigger excitement, curiosity must first be aroused: a sense that there is something to be discovered, that you are entering unexplored territory. Visitors must be amazed – before the familiar miracles of the BMW brand convey their message of reliability. What this suggests, founded on a great tradition, is that BMW is always a step ahead of the competition. Especially in relation to the more conservative Mercedes brand, BMW should be presented as young, fearless, dynamic.

A synthesis of technology and nature

The visitor moves through flowing spaces and forms set into the parkscape of the Olympic Park. Here it becomes strikingly clear that technology, in its most sophisticated form, is at one with the beauty of nature. The architecture we have developed for BMW is no longer the rigid architecture of mechanical reproduction. On the contrary – we are striving for an architecture of organic variations, an architecture that can adapt to the landscape and express all the variety of its context. A stimulating diversity of moods and spatial themes can be articulated through this organically varied architectural language, without creating an impression of disunity. In fact the opposite is true: despite the abundance of variation, the dominant impression is one of organic unity. The latest computer-aided production methods have allowed the construction industry, too, to move towards a paradigm of quasi-natural variations – getting ever closer to the beauty of the natural world.

Zaha Hadid

Atmosphäre und ästhetische Botschaft

Das BMW Erlebnis- und Auslieferungszentrum soll die Übergabe des neuen Wagens an den Kunden als ein unvergessliches Erlebnis inszenieren. Die Premium-Positionierung der Marke BMW impliziert ein hohes Erwartungsniveau, das es hier zu erfüllen gilt. Die Faszination des Besuchers verlangt mehr als nur gediegene Funktionserfüllung. Hier ist eine überraschende Serie von Raumerlebnissen gefragt, als Bühne für die Dramaturgie der Kundenbetreuung. Um ein Spannungsmoment aufzubauen, muss Neugier geweckt werden: Hier gibt es etwas zu entdecken, hier wird Neuland betreten. Es darf gestaunt werden, bevor die vertrauten Wunderwerke der Marke BMW das Gefühl von Verlässlichkeit vermitteln. Auf der Basis einer großen Tradition wird hier suggeriert: BMW ist der Konkurrenz immer einen Schritt voraus. Besonders gegenüber der eher konservativen Marke Mercedes ist BMW als jung, unerschrocken und dynamisch zu profilieren.

Eine Synthese aus Technik und Natur

Der Besucher bewegt sich durch die fließenden Räume und Formen, eingebettet in die Parklandschaft des Olympischen Gartens. Hier wird sinnfällig, dass Technik in ihrer höchsten Ausformulierung mit der Schönheit der Natur harmoniert. Die Architektur, die wir für BMW entwickeln, ist nicht mehr die starre Architektur der mechanischen Reproduktion. Vielmehr streben wir eine Architektur der organischen Variationen an, die es vermag, sich dem Terrain anzupassen und den ganzen Reichtum ihres Kontextes zu vermitteln. Eine belebende Vielfalt von Richtungen und Raumbedingungen kann mittels dieser organisch variierenden Architektursprache artikuliert werden, ohne dass ein Eindruck der Zerrissenheit entsteht. Ganz im Gegenteil, trotz Abwechslungsreichtum dominiert der Eindruck organischer Einheit. Die neuen computergesteuerten Produktionsmethoden machen auch in der Bauindustrie den Übergang zu einem Paradigma der naturähnlichen Variation möglich, in immer weiterer Annäherung an die Schönheit der Natur.

Zaha Hadid

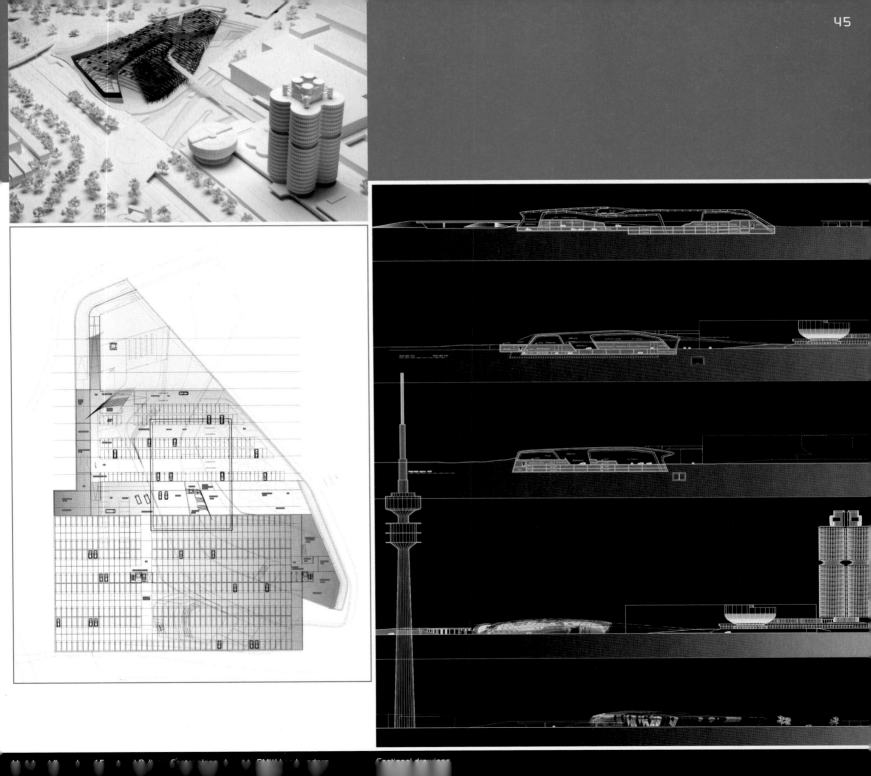

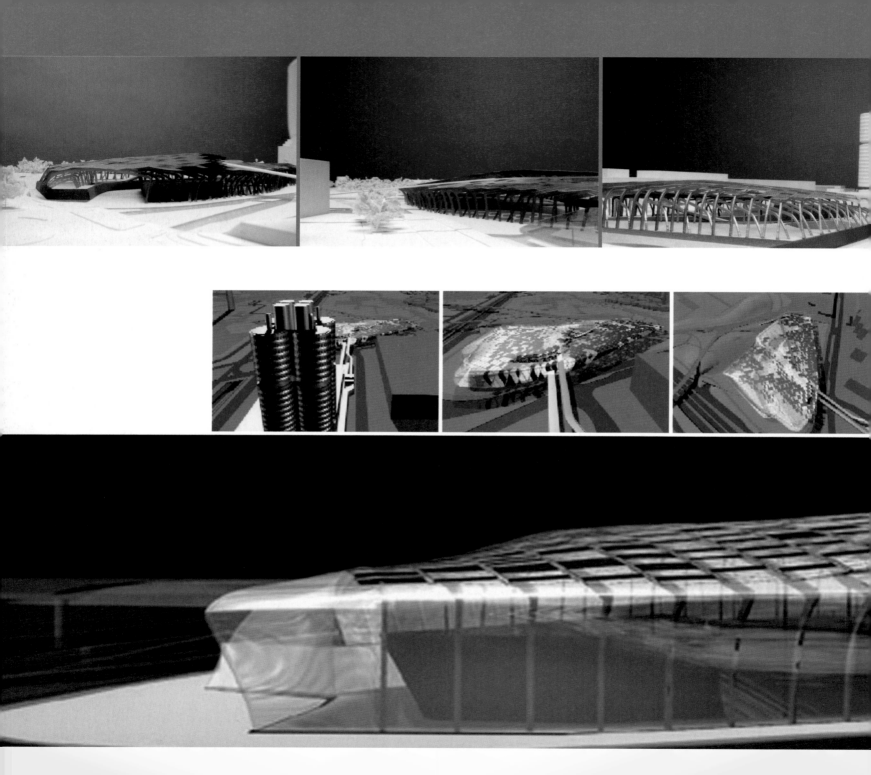

Interior views (top); exterior view (middle)
Innenansichten (oben); Außenansicht (Mitte)

Exterior view with car ramps (bottom)
Außenansicht mit Fahrzeugrampen (unten)

4th prize | 4. Preis: Morphosis Thom Mayne

Architectural narrative

The proposed scheme for the BMW Event and Delivery Center in Munich began as a metaphorical exploration of the experiential qualities of motoring freely on sinuously carved roadways in a finely tuned, precise machine. Ours is an integrative concept that weaves disparate parts of the existing urban fabric together with smooth, large-scale gestures evocative of fluidity and movement. The BMW Event Center responds to its context as a strong, recognizable landmark integrated seamlessly into its surroundings, complementing but not overwhelming the historically significant buildings that make up the BMW campus and the Olympic Park.

The design solution weaves together the existing and new circulation paths across the site. These paths of travel are then developed into a complex pattern of nodes and connections latent within the existing grid of the site. Within the design concept, the programmatic distinctions between the Premiere and the BMW World have been respected by carefully controlling both access and views. By locating much of the program at sub-ground levels we were able to recognize the dynamic, organic forms in the places where program and circulation systems intersect. The plan emphasizes interconnection between functions, a visual and physical legibility expressed in the principal axes. The resulting design has a sense of having evolved naturally and fluidly while remaining focused on its primary purpose: reinforcing the core values of BMW.

Morphosis Thom Mayne

Architektonische Beschreibung

Das vorgeschlagene Gebäude für das BMW Erlebnis- und Auslieferungszentrum in München entstand aus der metaphorischen Untersuchung der Wahrnehmungen während einer freien Fahrt auf gewundenen Straßen in einer fein abgestimmten, präzisen Maschine. Unser Konzept integriert die verschiedenen Elemente des bestehenden Stadtraums mittels einer geschmeidigen, großmaßstäblichen Geste, die Bewegung suggeriert. Das BMW Erlebnis- und Auslieferungszentrum präsentiert sich in seiner Umgebung als ein einprägsames Monument, welches sich zwischen den umliegenden historisch bedeutsamen Gebäuden des BMW-Komplexes und des Olympia-Stadions einfügt und diese zugleich ergänzt.

Der Entwurfsvorschlag verbindet die vorhandenen und die neu geplanten Verkehrswege auf dem gesamten Grundstück. Diese Wegverbindungen werden im Weiteren zu einem System von Verbindungspunkten innerhalb des bestehenden Gefüges entwickelt. Die programmatische Differenzierung zwischen dem Premiere-Bereich und der BMW World wird durch gezielte Kontrolle der Wegeführung und Blickbeziehungen erreicht. Indem ein großer Anteil des Programms im Untergeschoss angeordnet ist, kann sich das Gebäude in den oberen Geschossen als Reaktion auf die Verschneidungen von Programm und Infrastruktur in einer dynamischen und organischen Formensprache entfalten. Der Grundriss betont die Verbindungen zwischen Funktionsbereichen als visuelle und physisch erfahrbare Hauptachsen. Der hieraus entstandene Entwurf hat sich selbstverständlich und fließend entwickelt und konzentriert sich zugleich auf sein wichtigstes Ziel: die Kernwerte der BMW Group zu unterstreichen.

Morphosis Thom Mayne

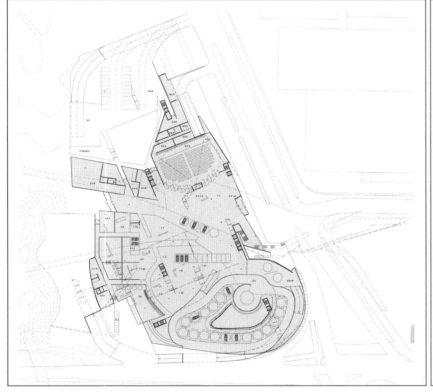

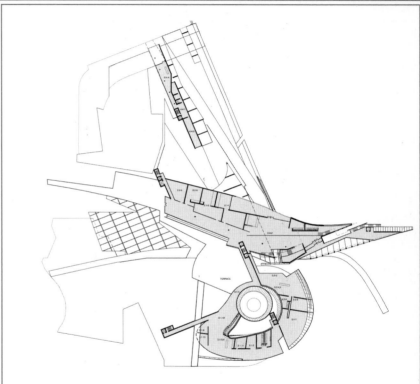

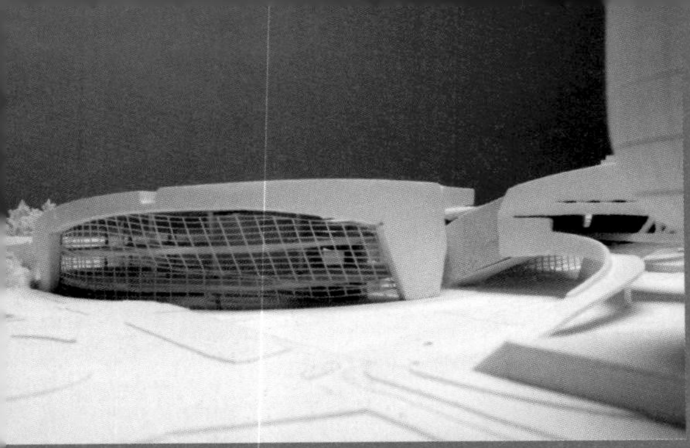

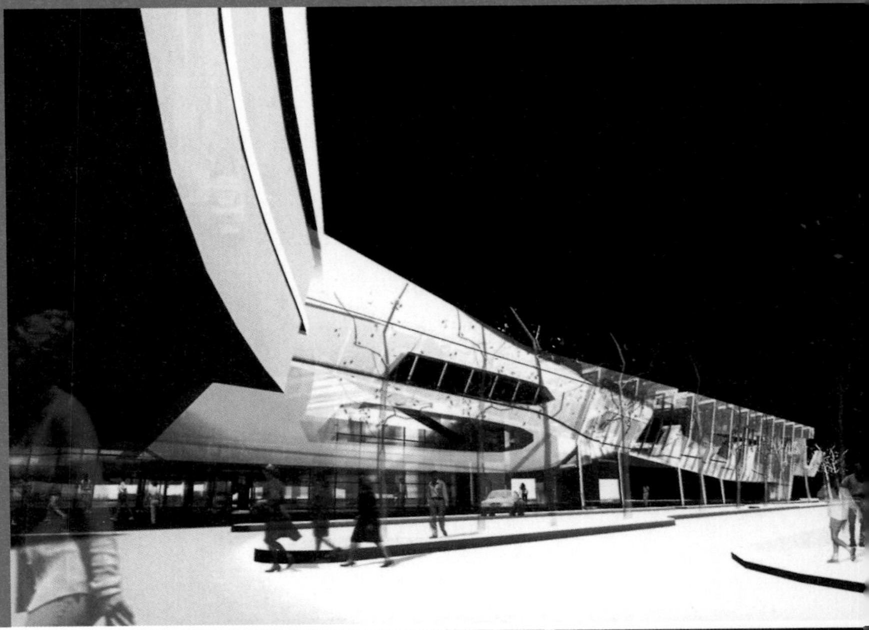

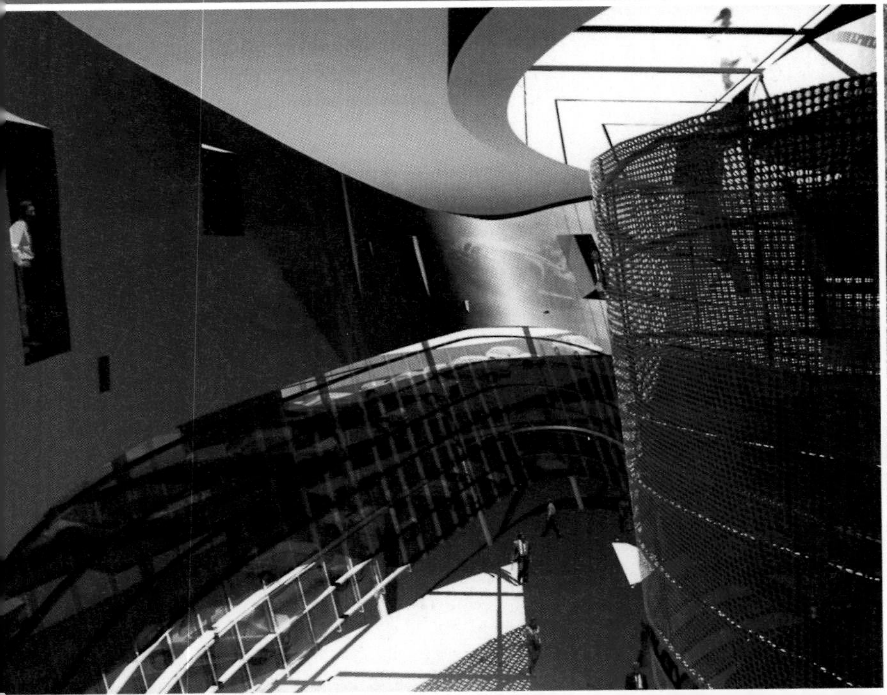

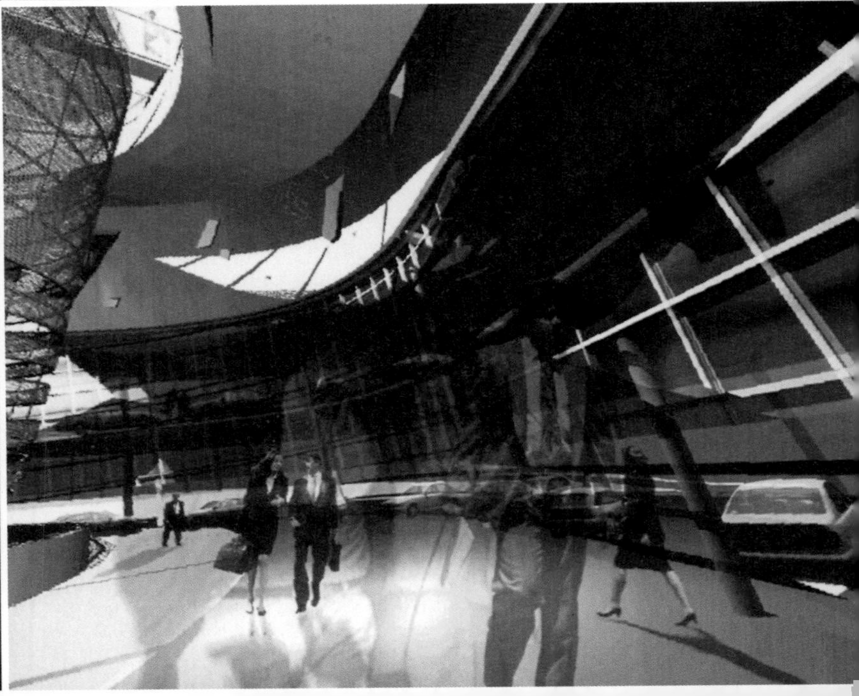

MALL BRANDING

VERKAUFSLAND-SCHAFT ALS MARKE

Mall branding

As the old adage has it: the three most important elements in retailing are location, location and location. Today that gem of wisdom needs a touch of modification, because the attractiveness of urban shopping spaces is subject to far-reaching change. Handed-down forms of retailing, not least the department store, are beating a retreat, leaving gaps in the cityscape to be filled by new hybrid projects like city malls. If these test-tube sales settings are to form an adequate stage for manufacturer and shop brands, they need to build a brand identity in their own right. One element of their successful marketing is their experience-oriented architecture. As the extensive revitalization projects at the main railway stations in Leipzig and Cologne illustrate to good effect, this can focus primarily on restoring the impressive historical substance of such items of infrastructural architecture. Alternatively, as in the new city malls in Düsseldorf and Erfurt, Germany, it can help to translate the legendary dream of the consumer temple into the modern age.

Verkaufslandschaft als Marke

Nur der Standort zählt, lautet eine alte Weisheit im Einzelhandel. Sie muss heute modifiziert werden. Denn die Attraktivität von urbanen Einkaufsarealen ist starken Veränderungen unterworfen. Tradierte Handelsformen, vor allem der Typus Kaufhaus, sind auf dem Rückzug, neue Hybridprojekte wie die City-Malls füllen innerstädtische Brachen. Solche Verkaufslandschaften aus der Retorte müssen, um zur Bühne für Hersteller- und Shopmarken zu werden, selbst Markencharakter ausbilden. Teil des erfolgreichen Marketings ist eine auf Erlebnisqualitäten setzende Architektur. Diese kann, wie in den aufwändigen Bahnhofsrevitalisierungen in Leipzig und Köln, in erster Linie auf die Wiedergewinnung der imponierenden historischen Substanz der Verkehrsbauten setzen. Sie kann aber auch, wie in den neuen City-Malls in Düsseldorf und Erfurt, dem legendären Traumbild des Konsumpalastes zur zeitgenössischen Entsprechung verhelfen.

Promenaden, Leipzig

Project | Projekt: Promenaden Hauptbahnhof Leipzig, 1998
Client | Bauherr: DB Immobilienfonds 7, Wieland KG, Hamburg,
        Deutsche Immobilien Anlagengesellschaft mbH
General planner and project management | Generalplaner und Projektmanagement: ECE Projekt-
        management G.m.b.H. & Co. KG
Architects | Architekten: HPP Hentrich-Petschnigg & Partner KG, Düsseldorf
        in Zusammenarbeit mit dem Bereich Architektur der ECE
Structural consultants | Tragwerksplanung: Kunkel und Partner, Düsseldorf/Leipzig
Project architects | Ausführungsplanung: Walter Bau-AG, Niederlassung Köln
        mit dbc Deutsche Bauconsulting GmbH, Düsseldorf, ARGE PSP Plan B, Düsseldorf,
        Ingenieurgesellschaft für Gebäudetechnik Skiba mbH, Herne, Seidl u. Partner, Regensburg
General contractor | Generalunternehmer: Walter Bau-AG, Niederlassung Köln, Walter Bau Sachsen G.m.b.H.

Leipzig's Hauptbahnhof (main railway station) is one of the city's largest and most important buildings. When it was officially opened in 1915 it was Europe's biggest railway station – an impressive symbol of the city's importance as a trade-fair centre and of the economic might of the German Reich. Today it still stands as one of Germany's most important works of transport architecture.

The Leipzig Hauptbahnhof 'Promenaden', a trend-setting retail and commercial centre set within the station, is the outcome of a pioneering railway station regeneration project. The aim of railway operator Deutsche Bahn AG is to re-establish Leipzig Hauptbahnhof as a focal point of urban life, by giving it a functional mix appropriate to its location, size and historic importance. The project includes both customer-oriented railway-specific functions and areas for commerce and retail, laying the foundations of a viable economic future for the station. The various uses and functions have been combined and balanced to create a multifunctional centre that is compatible with the historic context of the existing railway building.

The planned restructuring and modernisation of the station will take account of the various interests of the railway operators, the city and the retail sector, but above all of the people/customers using the building, giving Leipzig a brilliant new attraction. For travellers and visitors the railway station will once again be the focal point of the city's life, a mobility hub, communication forum and leisure centre – a place with an inviting atmosphere, a place people want to linger in and enjoy. The

Der Hauptbahnhof Leipzig ist eines der größten und wichtigsten Bauwerke der Stadt Leipzig und war bei seiner Einweihung 1915 größter Bahnhof Europas, der die Bedeutung der Messestadt und die wirtschaftliche Stärke des Deutschen Reiches repräsentieren sollte. Er gilt als eines der bedeutendsten deutschen Verkehrsbauwerke.

Die Promenaden Hauptbahnhof Leipzig, ein beispielgebendes Einkaufs- und Dienstleistungszentrum im Bahnhof, sind das Ergebnis eines Pilotprojektes in der Bahnhofsrevitalisierung. Die Deutsche Bahn AG möchte den Hauptbahnhof Leipzig wieder zu einem Mittelpunkt städtischen Lebens machen, indem sie ihm eine seiner Lage, Größe und historischen Bedeutung angemessene Nutzung gibt. Hierzu sollen neben kundenorientierten, bahnspezifischen Nutzungen Flächen für kommerzielle Dienstleistungen und Handel entstehen, die eine tragfähige wirtschaftliche Zukunft des Hauptbahnhofes ermöglichen. Die Art und Mischung dieser Nutzungen – der Branchenmix – soll so abgestimmt werden, dass ein "multifunktionales Zentrum" entsteht, das mit dem historischen Kontext des bestehenden Bahnhofsgebäudes verträglich ist.

Die geplante Umstrukturierung und Modernisierung des Hauptbahnhofs wird sowohl den Interessen der Bahn, der Stadt, des Handels sowie vor allem auch der Menschen/Kunden Rechnung tragen und ein neues Glanzlicht in Leipzig setzen. Für Reisende und Besucher soll der Bahnhof wieder zum Mittelpunkt des städtischen Lebens, zur Drehscheibe für Mobilität, zu einem Kommunikations- und Erlebniszen-

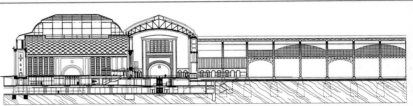

'Promenaden' will add a new retail and leisure centre with around 140 retail outlets – covering a total of 30,000 square metres – to the existing retail facilities in the city centre.

A new two-storey construction is planned beneath the station's transverse platform. These new floors will house vehicle and pedestrian infrastructure, and retail and commercial outlets along with the relevant ancillary services. The floor of the transverse platform will have large circular openings incorporating stairways, escalators, moving walkways and lifts connecting the different levels. Two architecturally attractive groups of lifts lead up to two platforms on the second floor; these will lead in turn to the satellite facilities planned for the second phase of the project. These 'satellites' will house the waiting areas for travellers using the ICE (high-speed train) platforms. Transparent membrane structures of steel and glass will be erected by the series of linked arches that separate the transverse platform from the other passenger platforms, in order to improve the climate on the transverse platform and on the levels below.

ECE Projektmanagement

trum werden – zu einem Ort mit einer einladenden Atmosphäre, die zum Verweilen anregt. Die Einkaufsmöglichkeiten in der Innenstadt werden mit den Promenaden um einen neuen Einkaufs- und Erlebnismittelpunkt mit etwa 140 Shops auf 30.000 Quadratmetern erweitert.

Unterhalb des Querbahnsteiges ist ein zweigeschossiger Neubaubereich vorgesehen. In diesen neuen Geschossen sollen Verkehrsflächen, Einzelhandels- und Dienstleistungs- einschließlich der dazugehörigen Nebenflächen untergebracht werden. Die Decke des Querbahnsteiges erhält großzügige, linsenförmige Öffnungen, in denen zur Verbindung der einzelnen Ebenen Treppenanlagen, Fahrtreppen, Fahrsteige sowie Aufzüge untergebracht werden. Über zwei architektonisch interessant gestaltete Aufzugsgruppen werden auch zwei Plattformen auf der Ebene des zweiten Obergeschosses erreicht, wo Übergänge an die im 2. Bauabschnitt vorgesehenen Satelliten angeordnet sind. In diesen Satelliten sollen die künftigen Aufenthaltsbereiche für Fernreisende im Bereich der ICE-Bahnsteige untergebracht werden. Im Bereich der Bogenbinderreihe, die den Querbahnsteig von den Längsbahnsteigen trennt, sollen transparente Membranen aus einer Glas-/Stahlkonstruktion angeordnet werden, um die klimatischen Bedingungen auf dem Querbahnsteig sowie in den darunterliegenden Geschossen zu verbessern.

ECE Projektmanagement

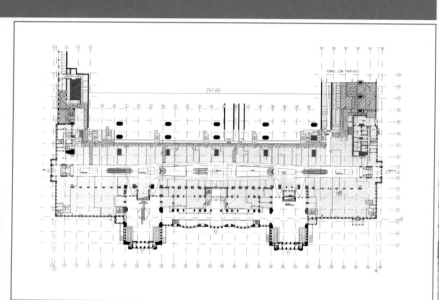

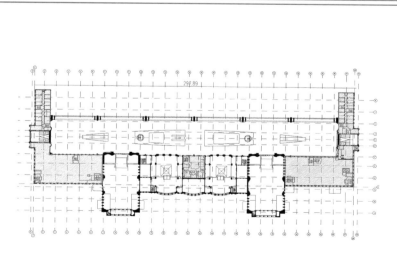

Floor plans main building and transverse platform, ground floor (top), mezzanine floor (bottom)

Entrance hall with new retail spaces

Lift tower of shopping mall

Colonaden, Cologne | Köln

Project | Projekt: Colonaden Köln Hbf, 2000
Client | Bauherr: Deutsche Bahn AG
General planner and project management | Generalplaner und Projektmanagement: ECE Projekt-
management
Architects | Architekten: OFFIS Architekten, Aachen; Bereich Architektur ECE
Project architects | Ausführungsplanung: OFFIS Architekten, Aachen, Pfeffer Architekten und Ingenieure
General contractor | Generalunternehmer: Heilit+Woerner Bau-AG

Cologne's Hauptbahnhof (main railway station) is one of the city's largest and most important buildings. Its location right at the heart of the city ensures excellent prospects for a new commercial centre including a high proportion of upmarket retail spaces. Parts of the building are over 100 years old, while others have been added at various stages over the intervening decades – with some modernization after sections of the station were destroyed in World War II. The regeneration project, transforming the station into a modern, upmarket centre for travel, communications and commerce, was designed to restore its prime importance as a focal point of city life.

At the same time, improving this core inner-city area also strengthens Cologne's position as a leading transport and communications centre. Cologne's Hauptbahnhof is one of Europe's key rail hubs. The station is the gateway to the city and a keystone in its central layout – encompassing the Cathedral, the Rhine, the Rhine bridge and the museums, as well as the Philharmonie (concert hall), Messe (trade fair complex), hotels and shopping streets – and so the design of the station and its surroundings is one of the city's most important urban design projects. The station's present-day appearance is the result of many new-build and conversion projects reflecting the ongoing adaptation of the architectural complex to the changing functions of the railway business.

In addition to customer-oriented railway-specific functions, the project will create areas for commercial and retail uses, laying the foundations of a viable economic future for the station. The functional mix will be designed to create a multifunctional centre – involving, in particular, the development of extensive disused spaces, such as the former luggage depot and the post office building, for commercial retail purposes. Beyond this, the railway-specific functions will be reorganised and effectively integrated within the overall mobility-station concept. Similarly, the upper storeys will see a change of use. Here the aim is to create a new and distinc-

Der Hauptbahnhof ist eines der größten und wichtigsten Bauwerke der Stadt Köln. Durch seine Lage im Zentrum der Stadt bietet er überzeugende Perspektiven für ein neues Dienstleistungszentrum mit einem bedeutendem Anteil qualitativ hochwertiger Einzelhandelsflächen. Das Bauwerk ist zum Teil über 100 Jahre alt und wurde im Laufe der Jahrzehnte immer wieder ergänzt und nach der teilweisen Zerstörung im Zweiten Weltkrieg zum Teil modernisiert. Durch die Revitalisierung zu einem modernen und qualitativ ansprechenden Mobilitäts-, Kommunikations- und Dienstleistungszentrum soll der Bahnhof seine Bedeutung als Mittelpunkt des städtischen Lebens wiedergewinnen.

Die Aufwertung dieses innerstädtischen Kernbereichs führt gleichzeitig auch zu einer Stärkung der Zentrumsfunktion der Stadt Köln. Der Kölner Hauptbahnhof ist einer der bedeutendsten Verkehrsknotenpunkte Europas. Als Entrée der Stadt und Schwerpunkt im städtebaulichen Gefüge Dom-Rhein-Rheinbrücke-Museen (Philharmonie, Messe, Hotels und Einkaufsstraßen eingeschlossen) gehört die Gestaltung des Hauptbahnhofes und seines Umfeldes zu den wichtigsten städtebaulichen Projekten Kölns. Zahlreiche Neu- und Umbaumaßnahmen, bedingt durch die ständige Anpassung des Gebäudekomplexes an die sich ändernden Funktionen des Bahnbetriebes, haben das heutige Erscheinungsbild des Hauptbahnhofes geprägt.

Die Umstrukturierung soll neben kundenorientierten, bahnspezifischen Nutzungen Flächen für kommerzielle Dienstleistungen und Handel entstehen lassen, die eine tragfähige wirtschaftliche Zukunft des Hauptbahnhofes ermöglichen. Die Art und Mischung dieser Nutzungen – der Branchenmix – soll so abgestimmt werden, dass ein "multifunktionales Zentrum" entsteht. Dazu sollen vor allem die großflächigen ungenutzten Räumlichkeiten – wie ehemaliger Gepäckdienst oder das Postgebäude – für den gewerblichen Einzelhandel ausgebaut werden. Außerdem ist geplant, die bahnspezifischen Nutzungen neu zu ordnen und schlüssig in das Gesamtkonzept Verkehrsstation zu integrieren. Desgleichen erfahren die Oberge-

tive identity for the railway station based on the symbiotic relationship of old and new – an identity that does justice to the city of Cologne in this historic location, directly alongside the Cathedral.

The overall design concept is based on the decision to widen Passage B to match the width of the open-plan Passage A, creating commercial retail units on either side of Passage B as well – and with the two passages connected by a spacious market hall on the site of the present luggage depot. The design of the market hall passage illustrates one of the key aims of the new design – creating a symbiosis of modern and historic architecture and restoring the full impact of the bridge construction for shoppers and travellers to enjoy. By inserting the retail architecture beneath the existing construction the architects have created not only a clear division between the loadbearing and non-loadbearing sections of the building but also an exciting interplay between old and new.

The façade on Breslauer Platz was redesigned to form part of the overall composition encompassing the platform roof structure, windbreak and façade. A second front elevation has been created here, complementing the redesigned entrances to passages A and B. High-quality materials and an innovative lighting concept create a bright, friendly atmosphere in the shopping area located beneath the platform level.

ECE Projektmanagement

schosse eine Umverlagerung ihrer Nutzung. Dabei bestehen die besonderen Herausforderungen und das Ziel darin, dem Bahnhof aus der Symbiose zwischen Alt und Neu eine unverwechselbare Identität zu verleihen, die insbesondere dem Standort Köln, an dieser geschichtsträchtigen Stelle neben dem Dom, angemessen Rechnung trägt.

Das Konzept basiert auf der Entscheidung, die B-Passage in ihrer Breite der einläufigen A-Passage anzupassen und ebenfalls beidseitig mit gewerblichem Einzelhandel zu versehen, wobei eine großzügige Markthalle auf der jetzigen Gepäckdienstfläche die Passagen miteinander verbindet. Der Entwurf der Markthallenpassage verdeutlicht eine der wesentlichen Aufgaben der Neugestaltung – die Symbiose zwischen moderner und historischer Architektur und die Wiedererlebbarkeit der Brückenkonstruktion für die Kunden und Reisenden. Durch das Hineinstellen der Ladenarchitektur in die vorhandene Konstruktion wird nicht nur den statischen Erfordernissen einer sauberen Trennung zwischen dynamisch belasteten und unbelasteten Bauteilen entsprochen, sondern es entsteht auch ein spannungsreiches Wechselspiel zwischen Alt und Neu.

Die Fassade am Breslauer Platz wurde als Element der Gesamtkomposition Bahnsteigüberdachung, Windschutz und Fassade überplant. In Ergänzung zu den neu gestalteten Eingängen der A- und B-Passage wird hier eine zweite Vorderseite geschaffen.

Hochwertige Materialien und innovatives Beleuchtungskonzept sorgen in dem Shopping-Bereich, der unter der Gleisebene angesiedelt ist, für eine helle und freundliche Atmosphäre.

ECE Projektmanagement

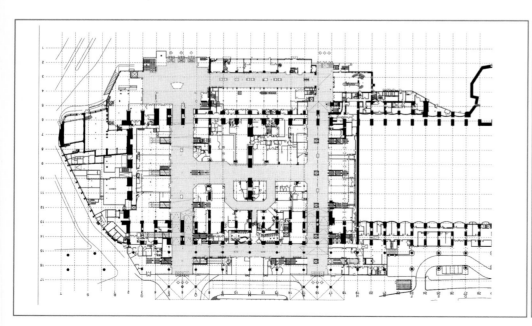

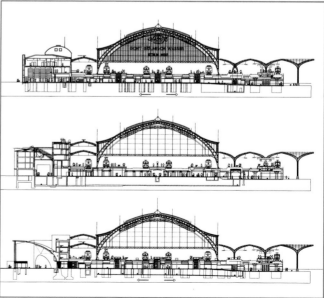

Sevens, Düsseldorf

Project | Projekt: Sevens, Düsseldorf, 2000
Client | Bauherr: Sevens Düsseldorf GbR
Architects | Architekten: RKW Architekten
Total costs | Ges. Baukosten: DM 85.000.000
Gross floor space | BGF: 35.700 m²
Usable floor space | HNF: 15.500 m²
Site | Grundstück, Planungsgebiet: Königsallee 56 – Steinstraße 5
Conceptual phase | Planungszeit: 1997 – 2000
Construction phase | Bauzeit: April 1999 – October 2000
Completion | Fertigstellung: 4.10.2000
Award | Auszeichnung: MIPIM Award 2001

The core of the Sevens Shopping Centre is a generous open space, which extends over seven levels and opens out towards the top. The glazed mall roof raises its outline over the roofs of the city and its glass mall façade apex provides a landmark on the Königsallee.

Horizontal shopping movements are transformed into vertical access. The themes of retail and changing consumer behaviour patterns demand high visibility and transparency. Natural light, reduced numbers of different materials used, and colour provide an appropriate ambience.

RKW Architekten

Kernstück des Sevens Shopping Centers bildet ein großzügiger Luftraum, der über sieben Ebenen reicht und sich nach oben aufweitet. Die gläserne Mallüberdachung, die den Grundriss über die Dächer der Stadt erhebt, wird mit der gläsernen Mallspitze in der Fassade zur Landmarke auf der Königsallee.

Horizontale Shopping-Bewegungen werden in vertikale Erschließung umgewandelt. Theme Retailing und wandelndes Konsumentenverhalten bedingen hohe Visibilität und Transparenz. Natürliches Licht, die reduzierte Materialwahl und Farbigkeit sorgen für ein entsprechendes Ambiente.

RKW Architekten

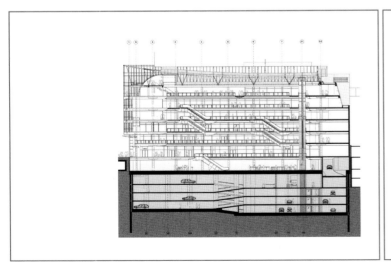

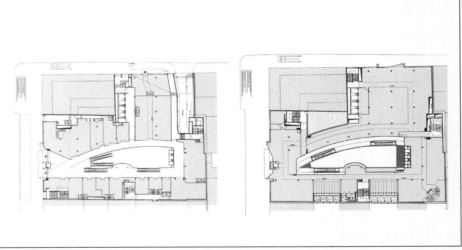

Atrium view: coffeeshop area
Blick in das Atrium: Cafébereich

Anger 1, Erfurt

Project | Projekt: Anger 1, Erfurt, 2000
Client | Bauherr: Optimus Grundstücksgesellschaft mbH & Co. Bauträger-KG
Architects | Architekten: RKW Architekten
Total costs approx. | Ges. Baukosten: ca. 79.500.000 DM
Gross floor space | BGF: 30.462 qm
Usable floor space | HNF: ca. 24.080 qm
Site | Grundstück, Planungsgebiet: 5.792 qm
Conceptual phase | Planungszeit: Januar 1998 – September 1998
Construction phase | Bauzeit: Oktober 1998 – September 2000
Completion | Fertigstellung: September 2000
Award | Auszeichnung: ISCS Recommendation 2001

In addition to renovating the historical "Römischer Kaiser" building in accordance with the ancient monument legislation, new buildings twice its size will be erected.

The mall stages a dramatization of restriction and expansion. The routes meet in a large covered rotunda, which allows daylight to enter right down to the basement. The historic light well in the old part was partially rebuilt and fitted with a new coloured glass luminous ceiling.

The new parts of the building present themselves externally as restrained in their materiality and form of language. The natural stone façade of the extension captures the proportions of the old building and transforms them into the present.

RKW Architekten

Neben dem historischen Gebäude „Römischer Kaiser" mit seiner Jugendstilfassade, das denkmalschutzgerecht saniert wird, entsteht ein doppelt so großer Neubau.

Die Mall folgt einer inszenierten Dramaturgie von Enge und Weite. Die Wege treffen sich in einer großen, überdachten Rotunde, die Tageslicht bis in das Untergeschoss fallen lässt. Der historische Lichthof im Altbau wurde teilweise wieder hergestellt und mit einer neuen farbigen Glas-Lichtdecke versehen.

Nach außen präsentieren sich die neuen Gebäudeteile in ihrer Materialität und Formensprache zurückhaltend. Die Natursteinfassade der Erweiterung greift die Proportionen des Altbaus auf und transformiert sie in die Gegenwart.

RKW Architekten

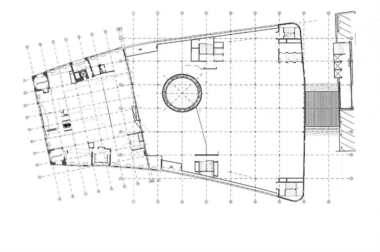

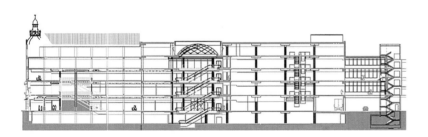

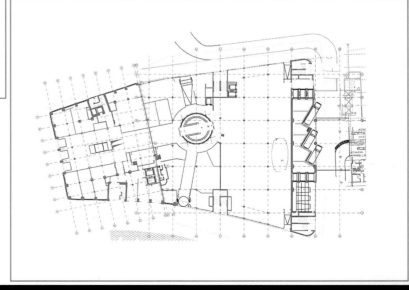

Anger 1: historical part with adjoining new department store (top); sectional drawing (bottom)

Floor plans fourth floor (top) and ground floor (bottom)

New atrium rotunda
Neues Rundatrium

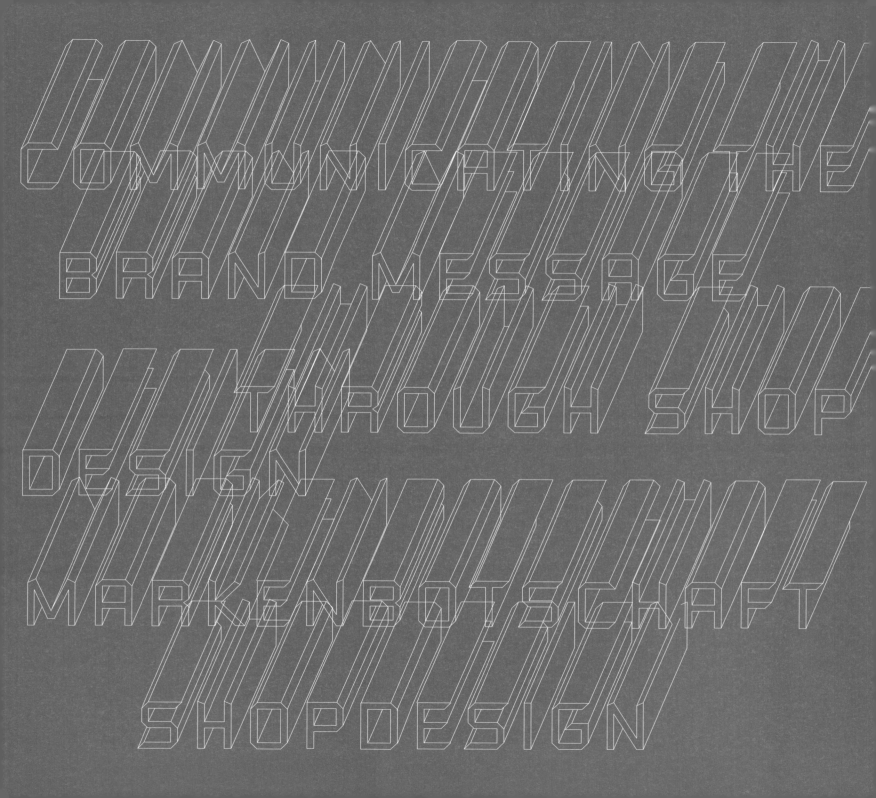

COMMUNICATING THE
BRAND MESSAGE
THROUGH SHOP
DESIGN

MARKENBOTSCHAFT
SHOPDESIGN

Communicating the brand message through shop design

Creating a readily multipliable form of brand identity ranks high on the list of specifications for modular shop design concepts. These must work in stand-alone and shop-in-shop settings alike by being readily recognizable to the customer. The design of the retail environment must merge with the brand image down to the finest details. Expressiveness, the purposeful use of characteristic forms, and calculated elements of surprise combine to form an integral whole. Wherever necessary, a change of scene from one area or season to the next should be built into these flexible brand worlds. Examples of shop design conveying the brand message include the real-world customer centres of an Internet bank; the dynamic 3D fantasy world created by a cult training shoe brand; the multimedia shops of a retail chain; the experience-oriented redefinition of hypermarkets; or the prototype of a new generation of cosmetics retail outlets geared to a single brand.

Markenbotschaft Shopdesign

Markenidentität, die sich multiplizieren lässt, ist Zielvorgabe für modulare Shopdesign-Konzepte. Sie müssen sowohl autonom wie als Shop-in-Shops durch hohe Wiedererkennbarkeit funktionieren. Die Gestaltung der Verkaufsumgebung verschmilzt bis ins Detail mit dem Markenbild. Expressivität, starker Formwillen, kalkulierte Überraschungsmomente bilden eine Einheit. Wo nötig, sollte auch der Szenenwechsel von Bereich zu Bereich oder von Saison zu Saison diesen flexiblen Markenwelten eingebaut sein. Beispiele für Shopdesign als Markenbotschaft sind: der reale Kundenzentren-Auftritt einer Internet-Bank; die dynamische dreidimensionale Fantasy-Welt einer Turnschuh-Kultmarke; die Multimedia-Läden einer Handelskette; die erlebnisorientierte Neudefinition von Einkaufsmärkten; der Prototyp einer neuen Generation von, auf eine Einzelmarke zugeschnittenen, Kosmetikfilialen.

Punto Mediolanum

Project | Projekt: Punto Mediolanum 1999
Client | Bauherr: Banca Mediolanum
Architects and interior designers | Architekten und Innenarchitekten: Massimo Iosa Ghini, Barbara Delucca
Lighting consultants | Lichtplanung: ZumtobelStaff Italia
Realization | Ausführung: Facco Pubblicità

In the financial world, the Internet has established itself for distance transactions. This makes the system faster and more efficient, but weakens the personal and professional relationships between bank and client. Banca Mediolanum, which has 5000 customer service agents, therefore decided to strengthen its presence and visibility on the ground. The project "Punto Mediolanum" was born, with the aim of opening more than 300 customer service centres throughout Italy.

Our task was to translate an existing, virtual operative structure into a real one, with a design that reflected the company's philosophy. The solution was contemporary in style, as well as being essential and elegant. The branches use high-tech materials such as aluminium to balance wood and natural stone, which embody values such as solidity and tradition.

Studio Iosa Ghini

In der Finanzwelt hat sich das Internet als Transaktionsplattform durchgesetzt. Systemeffizienz und Schnelligkeit sind seine Vorteile. Aber zugleich wird die persönliche und fachliche Verbindung zwischen Bank und Kunde geschwächt. Deshalb entschied sich die Internet-Bank Mediolanum, für ihre 5.000 Kundenberater die Präsenz und Wahrnehmbarkeit an realen Orten zu erhöhen. Das war der Ausgangspunkt des Projekts Punto Mediolanum mit dem Ziel, mehr als 300 Beratungsfilialen in ganz Italien zu eröffnen.

Als Entwurfsaufgabe stellte sich die Übersetzung und Ausarbeitung einer schon existenten, virtuellen, operativen Unternehmensstruktur in eine der Firmenphilosophie entsprechende Gestaltungsqualität. Das Ergebnis war eine sehr zeitgemäße, aber zugleich auf das Wesentliche konzentrierte und elegante Lösung. Das Filialsystem nutzt technologische Materialien wie Aluminium im Ausgleich zu Holz und Naturstein, die eher Solidität und Tradition verkörpern.

Studio Iosa Ghini

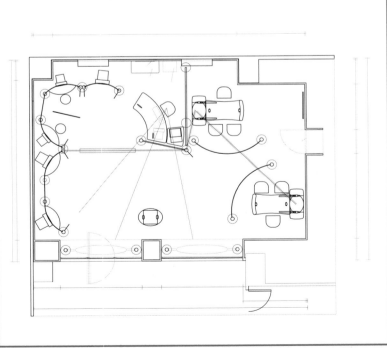

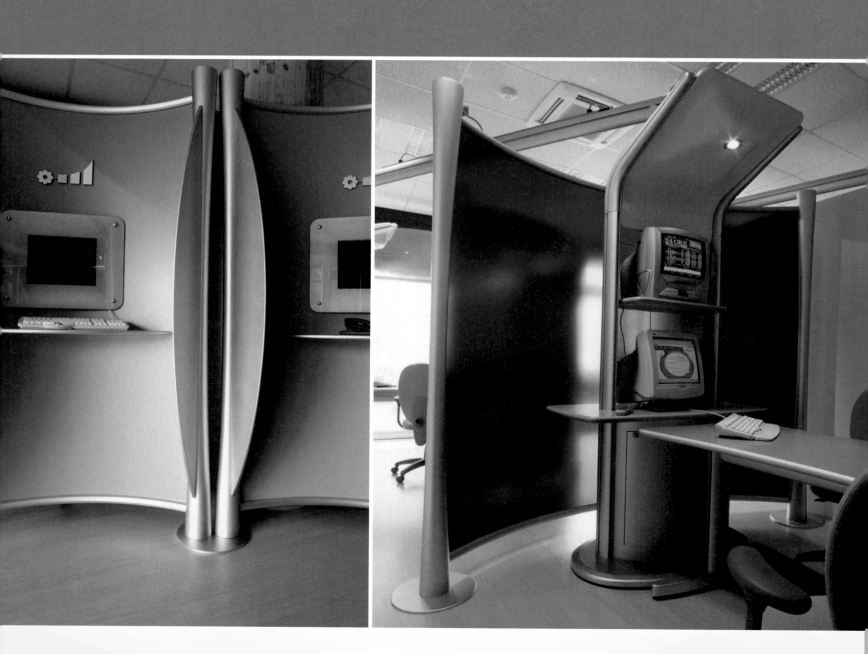

Conference area Punto Mediolanum
Besprechungsbereich Punto Mediolanum

Superga

Project | Projekt: Superga Store System, 1998
Client | Bauherr: Superga
Architects and interior designers | Architekten und Innenarchitekten: Massimo Iosa Ghini, Marco Frignani
Realization | Ausführung: Lisar Arredamenti

Since 1911, all the Superga company's activities have revolved around rubber. The branch achieved international renown for a number of products, but principally for its canvas shoes. All that was needed to give it the decisive push into cult status was the requisite retail ambience, and in 1996 our studio was engaged for this purpose.

In this case the key task was not just to sell products but also to convey a new brand message. This led us to move away from the term "shop" and to think increasingly of a "mediological gallery", where people go not just to buy a quality product, but also to discover the culture of quality that generated it.

We therefore designed the shop with back-lit screens, as carriers of graphics, communication and the product itself. We defined a key material, rubber, as Superga's primary medium for communicating with its customers on an aesthetic and emotional level. Rubber is omnipresent in the store concept, which can be applied as a modular display system or a complete interior. Rubber on the walls and translucent shelves, rubber-coated fabrics for the seating, rubber in the form of latex paints used for all the fittings, even rubber in liquid form in the upholstery.

Larger-scale Superga stores following this format were initially set up in Italian cities and later on in European capitals.

Studio Iosa Ghini

Seit 1911 steht Gummi im Mittelpunkt der Aktivitäten des Unternehmens Superga. Internationale Anerkennung erreichte die Marke mit einer ganzen Reihe von Produkten, vor allem aber mit ihren Sportschuhen aus Leinen. Was bisher fehlte, um Superga den entscheidenden Schub hin zum Kultstatus zu geben, war das notwendige Shop-Umfeld. Dieses zu entwickeln, wurden wir 1996 beauftragt.

Schlüsselaufgabe war in diesem Fall nicht der Verkauf von Produkten, sondern die Vermittlung einer neuen Markenbotschaft. Das führte dazu, dass wir auf den Leitbegriff „Verkaufsgeschäft" verzichteten und stattdessen mehr und mehr in Richtung einer „mediologischen Galerie" dachten, wo man nicht nur hingeht, um ein Qualitätsprodukt zu erwerben, sondern um zugleich die hinter der Ware stehende Qualitätskultur zu erfahren.

Aus diesen Grünen wurde das Shop-System mit hinterleuchteten Wandschirmen entwickelt, die Träger für Grafiken, Kommunikation und für das Produktangebot sind. Außerdem definierten wir auf ästhetischer und emotionaler Ebene ein Kernmaterial, Gummi, als Supergas primäres Medium der Kundenansprache. Gummi ist omnipräsent im gesamten Shop-Konzept, das sich als modularer Teileinbau wie auch als komplette Ladeneinrichtung einsetzen lässt. Gummi wurde verwendet als Wandbelag und für transluzente Regale, als textiler Bezug für die Sitzmöbel, als Latexfarbe, als Polstermaterial.

Das Shop-Konzept wurde zunächst mit Superga Stores in allen größeren italienischen Städten realisiert und danach in den europäischen Metropolen.

Studio Iosa Ghini

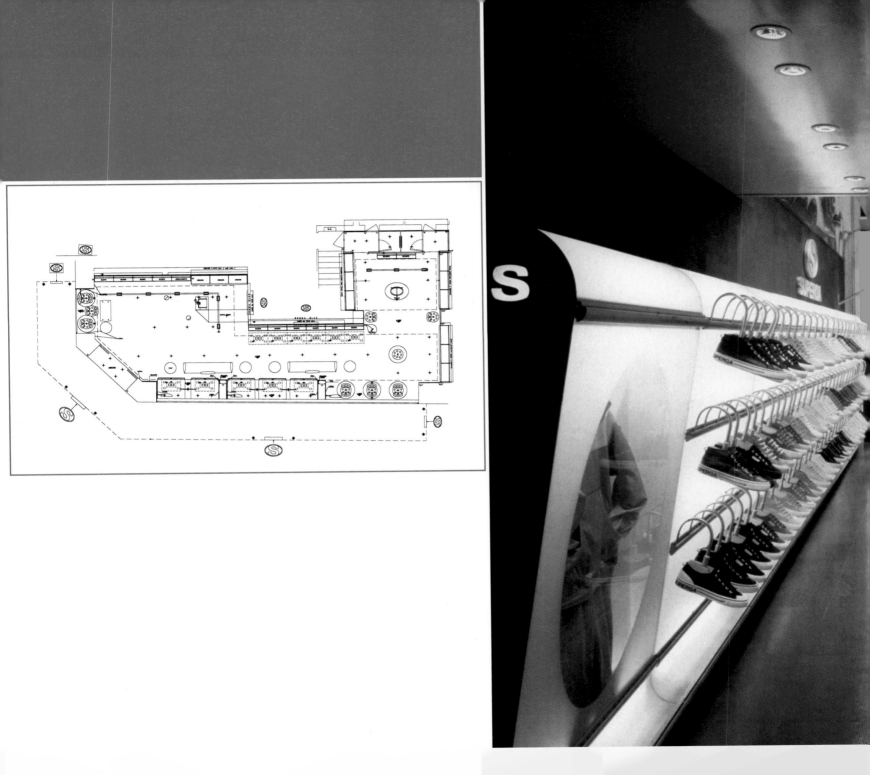

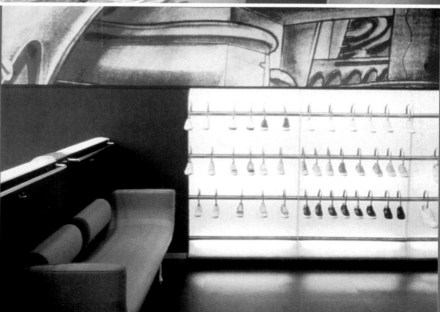

Interior view Superga Store (top); detail lighting system (bottom)

Display system apparel (top); seating area (bottom)

Display area shoes in front of back-lighting screen

Esselunga

Project | Projekt: Esselunga AudioVideoFoto, 2001
Client | Bauherr: Esselunga
Architects and interior designers | Architekten und Innenarchitekten: Massimo Iosa Ghini, Marco Frignani
Consultant | Planung: Davide Ortolani
Realization | Ausführung: Sangiorgi

Our briefing was to design a shop selling hi-fi and electronic products, within the big department store Esselunga. The Esselunga trademark and logo are developing into a soft, sober and soft-modern aesthetic, integrating the values of tradition and modernity.

On the other hand, the aesthetic of the media/technological world tends towards advanced models that favour streamlined shapes, communicating modernity and future.

The appearance of our Media Store was therefore characterized by an image that is more appealing and closer to the aesthetic of the product. We nevertheless adhered to the guidelines of the trademark, for example by using the same floor as in the surrounding shops and by maintaining a certain essentiality of style, so that our contemporary interpretation always recalls the mother company Esselunga.

Studio Iosa Ghini

Die Aufgabenstellung lautete, eine spezielle Verkaufsfläche für Unterhaltungs- und Kommunikationselektronik innerhalb der großen Esselunga-Einkaufsmärkte zu entwerfen. Die Handelsmarke und das Logo Esselunga entwickeln sich hin zu einer weichen, nüchternen und sacht-modernen Ästhetik, welche die Werte von Tradition und Modernität gleichermaßen einschließt.

Auf der anderen Seite tendiert die Ästhetik der Welt der Medientechnologie hin zu futuristischen, stromlinienförmigen Modellen, die für Modernität und Zukunft stehen.

Das Erscheinungsbild unseres Media Store wurde deshalb durch ein Image geprägt, das sowohl ansprechender als auch besser auf den Produktcharakter zugeschnitten ist. Gleichzeitig hielten wir uns jedoch an die Richtlinien der Handelsmarke. Dazu gehören etwa die Anpassung des Fußbodens an den der übrigen Verkaufsumgebung und die Wahrung eines gewissen Grundstils, der bei aller Neuinterpreation von Zeitgemäßheit immer an die Muttergesellschaft Esselunga erinnert.

Studio Iosa Ghini

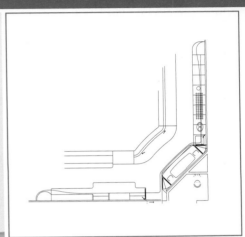

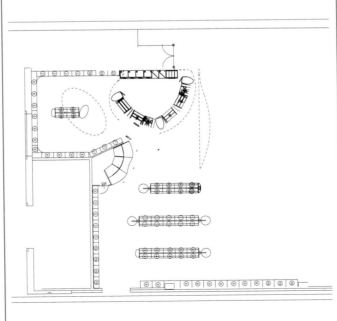

Audio Video Foto

CAD drawing rack systems

Migros

Project | Projekt: Migros Store System, 2000
Client | Bauherr: Migros AG
Architect, interior designer, retail concept | Architekt, Innenarchitekt, Ladenkonzept: Jos de Vries,
       The Retail Company

Through expansion and international growth, today's retail groups have developed into highly professional operations pursuing business strategies that tend to focus on two main goals: achieving rational, process-oriented operational management based on optimised logistics, cost control and efficiency; and on the customer side, achieving more effective shop branding by using marketing and communications techniques optimally and by creating emotionally effective retail environments. The retail space is subject to constant change, so it has to be flexible, responsive, efficient and self-contained – always capable of surprising the customers who use it.

As retail designers, our aim is constantly to renew the customers' attachment to our client's brand through captivating, innovative ideas, and at the same time to remain one step ahead of the competition through our knowledge of market risks and opportunities. To be successful, a retail concept needs to do more than just implement the various marketing tools correctly. These rational starting points must be converted into effective shop branding with a strong emotional component, through careful positioning and effective communications.

From shop concept to shop brand, from commercial identity to brand personality: that was the philosophy behind our radical repositioning of Migros. Migros makes a key contribution to the quality of life in Switzerland and aims to be seen as a dependable partner in this context. Its image is that of a well-organized, broad-based, innovative, responsible, likeable, practical and customer-friendly group. These characteristics form the basis for developing the ethos of the corporate identity, as experienced in each individual retail outlet.

Durch Maßstabsvergrößerung und Internationalisierung haben sich die Einzelhandelsorganisationen zu professionellen Unternehmen entwickelt, deren Geschäftspolitik oftmals zwei Hauptziele verfolgt: Zum einen wird eine rationelle, prozessorientierte Betriebsführung mit optimaler Logistik, Kostensenkung und Effizienz angestrebt. Zum anderen wird, was die Kundenseite anbelangt, durch optimalen Einsatz von Marketing- und Kommunikationstechniken und emotionale Erlebnisdimensionen auf verstärktes Shop Branding gesetzt. Die Verkaufsfläche ist einem ständigen Wandel unterworfen, sie muss deshalb flexibel, schnell umbaubar, effizient und eigenständig sein und den Kunden immer wieder aufs Neue überraschen.

Als Retail Designer wollen wir die Kunden unserer Auftraggeber durch innovative und verblüffende Ideen immer wieder aufs Neue binden, aber auch durch die Kenntnis von Marktchancen und -risiken der Konkurrenz immer einen Schritt voraus sein. Der Erfolg eines Shop-Konzepts erfordert mehr als nur die richtige Anwendung der Marketinginstrumente. Diese rationalen Ausgangspunkte müssen über eine ausgewogene Positionierung und eine richtige Kommunikation in ein Shop Branding mit emotionalem Erlebnis umgesetzt werden.

Vom Shop-Konzept zur Shop-Marke, von der Geschäftsidentität zur Markenpersönlichkeit: Das war unser Grundgedanke für die groß angelegte Neupositionierung von Migros. Migros trägt zur Lebensqualität in der Schweiz bei und möchte in diesem Punkt ein verlässlicher Partner sein. Das Image ist das eines gut organisierten, breit orientierten, innovativen, verantwortungsbewussten, sympathischen, praktischen und kundenfreundlichen Konzerns. Diese Merkmale bildeten den Grund-

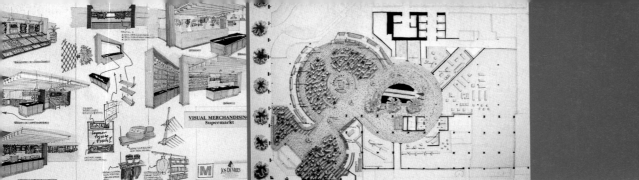

This is the place where customers make their purchasing decision – the place that must trigger this decision. And so it is here, where the retailer communicates with its customers, that the brand's positioning must be put across clearly. The tools at the retailer's disposal begin with the shop front – this invites the customer to come in. An effective layout guides the customer effectively around the shop, while the shop design and graphic communications, the materials and colours used create a pleasant atmosphere and the visual merchandising prompts spontaneous purchases. Alongside the optimum combination of these different tools, the coordination of in-store communications with external communications is also a crucial factor. The image must match the retail experience.

For the Migros corporate identity, we chose a light, clear and welcoming layout. Each department has its own distinctive ambience, although a common thread runs through all of them, ensuring a unified overall effect. The key issue is maintaining the overall identity, while striking the optimum balance between commerce, culture and authenticity, between product and consumer, between colour and material – across all product groups. The new overall concept communicates the Migros ethos: warm, bright, positive, varied, surprising, clearly organized, modern, practical, high-quality.

Jos de Vries

gedanken für die Entwicklung der Seele der Unternehmensidentität, erlebbar in der einzelnen Verkaufsfiliale.

Hier ist der Ort der Kaufentscheidung, zu der der Kunde veranlasst werden soll. Und so muss hier, wo der Einzelhändler mit seinem Kunden kommuniziert, die Marke klar vermittelt werden. Das erste Mittel hierfür ist die Geschäftsfront – sie lädt den Kunden ein. Durch ein gutes Layout wird er innen effektiv geführt, das Shop-Design und die grafische Kommunikation, die eingesetzten Materialien und die Farbgebung schaffen eine angenehme Atmosphäre und das Visual Merchandising verleitet zu Spontankäufen. Neben der optimalen Ausrichtung dieser Mittel ist die Abstimmung zwischen der Instore-Kommunikation und der externen Kommunikation von wesentlicher Bedeutung. Image und Shop-Erlebnis müssen übereinstimmen.

Zur Corporate Identity von Migros wurde ein helles, übersichtliches und niedrigschwelliges Layout gewählt. Jede Abteilung hat ihr eigenes Ambiente, jedoch verbindet ein roter Faden alle Bereiche zu einer Einheit. Das Thema lautet: die Wahrung des Ganzen und die Suche nach dem richtigen Verhältnis zwischen Kommerz, Kultur und Ursprünglichem, zwischen Produkt und Konsument, zwischen Farbe und Material – und zwar für alle Produktgruppen. Das neue Gesamtkonzept kommuniziert das Migros-Gefühl: warm, hell, fröhlich, abwechslungsreich, überraschend, übersichtlich, modern, praktisch, qualitätvoll.

Jos de Vries

Escalator connecting ground and first floor (top); served food counter (middle)

Interior views with served (middle) and self-service counters (bottom)

Migros food court

Bakery area (top); rack corridor (middle); fruit and vegetable area (bottom)

Qiora

Project | Projekt: Qiora Store and Spa, Madison Avenue, New York, 2000
Client | Bauherr: Shiseido Cosmetics
Architect | Architekten: Architecture Research Office (ARO)
ARO project team | Projektteam: Stephen Cassell and Adam Yarinsky (partners in charge)
        Scott Abrahams (project architect), Josh Pulver, Eunice Seng, Rosalyne Shieh, Kim Yao.
Art director and designer | Artdirektor und Designer: Roshi Kudo, Shiseido Creative
Structural consultant | Statik: Selnick/Harwood Consulting Engineers PC
Mechanical engineer | Technik: Lilker Associates
Lighting consultant | Lichtdesign: Johnson Schwinghammer Lighting Consultants, Inc.
Curtain consultant | Textildesign: Mary Bright, Inc.
Audio-visual consultant | AV-Design: Shen Milsom and Wilke
Owner's representative | Projektsteuerung Bauherr: Hiroko Sueyoshi Planners

Located on Madison Avenue, the Qiora Store and Spa Introduces Shiseido's new skin care product line to North America. The Qiora brand is presented as a unique sensory experience that unites the product with the space, transforming the conventional act of shopping. A new conception of forms, materials, and lighting creates a calm, glowing landscape that is visually open to the sidewalk.

Form

Curvilinear shapes create a continuity as space that encourages exploration. Three cylindrical spa cabins float in plan, blurring the boundary between the retail and spa areas. To preserve the openness of the interior, the service rooms are located in a cluster along the south edge of the 140-square-metre space.

Materials

Hard surfaces are veiled in suspended translucent organza panels. As visitors circulate through the space, layers of fabric panels continually reconfigure collages of colour and light. In the retail area, the fabric creates soft boundaries for consultation and reception. In the spa area, fabric shrouds the more intimate spaces of the lounge

Am Standort Madison Avenue führt Qiora Store and Spa die neue Kosmetikpflegelinie für Nordamerika ein. Die Marke Qiora wird präsentiert als eine einzigartige Sinneserfahrung, basierend auf der Einheit von Produkt und Raum, die den konventionellen Kaufakt transformiert. Ein neues Form-, Material- und Lichtkonzept schafft eine ruhige, leuchtende Landschaft, die sich visuell zum Straßenraum öffnet.

Formensprache

Geschwungene Formen bilden ein Raumkontinuum, das zu Erkundungen einlädt. Drei zylindrische Behandlungskabinen schweben im Raum und heben die Grenze zwischen Verkaufs- und Behandlungsbereich auf. Um den offenen Charakter des Interieurs zu erhalten, wurden die Serviceräume am südlichen Rand der 140 Quadratmeter großen Fläche zusammengefasst.

Materialien

Harte Oberflächen werden verhüllt mit abgehängten, transluzenten Organza-Textilfeldern. Während die Kunden sich durch den Raum bewegen, konfigurieren diese Schichten von Textilfeldern ständig wechselnde Collagen aus Farbe und Licht. Im Ver-

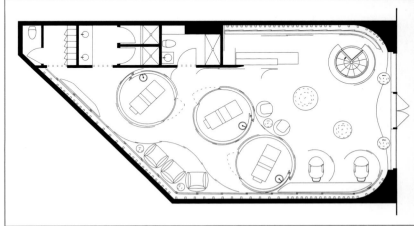

and cabins. The walls of the cabins are opaque and lined with ultra suede, creating a soft and quiet place for relaxation.

Lighting

In this space, light is a material. The environment is lit by dimmed and fabric-diffused perimeter fluorescent lighting, with no distracting light fixtures visible. The light modulates between warm and cool shades to create a sensation of daylight and a radiant glow on the skin. Similarly, the product is always experienced in the softness of light and fabric. The product glows on display fixtures with fibre-optic uplights that cycle through shades of white during the day and blue at night. At night, the store is a lantern to the outside.

Architecture Research Office

kaufsbereich sorgen die Stoffe für weiche Abgrenzungen zwischen Empfang und Beratung. Im Behandlungsbereich umgeben Stoffe die intimeren Flächen der Lounge und der Behandlungskabinen. Die Wände der Kabinen sind opak und ausgekleidet mit Ultra-Wildleder, was einen weichen und ruhigen Ort der Entspannung schafft.

Beleuchtung

In diesem Raum wird Licht zum Material. Das Ambiente beleuchten gedimmte, vom Stoff verdeckte, rundum verteilte Leuchtstoffröhren; keinerlei ablenkende Leuchte ist sichtbar. Das Licht wechselt zwischen warmen und kühlen Tönen, ahmt so den Eindruck von Tageslicht nach und schafft ein strahlendes Leuchten auf der Haut. In ähnlicher Weise begegnet man dem Produkt in der Sanftheit von Licht und Stoff. Die Produkte selbst erstrahlen auf Displayflächen mit Glasfiber-Uplights, die tagsüber in verschiedenen Weißtönen, nachts in Blau leuchten. In der Nacht wirkt der Quiora Store zur Straße hin wie eine einzige Laterne.

Architecture Research Office

Product display wall

Brandscaping

New dimensions in retail design. An expert roundtable
Neue Wege im Retail-Design. Workshop-Diskussion
mit Experten

Participants: John Hoke, Global Creative Director Nike Brand Design, Beaverton, USA, Massimo Iosa Ghini, architect and designer, Bologna, Italy, Jens Kalkbrenner, architect, ECE Hamburg, Johannes Ringel, architect, RKW Architekten, Düsseldorf

Moderators: Burkhard Fröhlich, editor-in-chief, DBZ, Gütersloh
Otto Riewoldt, architectural journalist, Cologne

_____Burkhard Fröhlich: What is the best way to create and plan a new dimension in retail design and brandscaping – from the viewpoint of Nike as a global brand, for example?

_____John Hoke: The most important thing for us before we process a new project is to understand what the consumer context is. We then try to provide a vision that helps lead the customer through – a vision that is relevant and resonates with the customer. Many of our design solutions are a step ahead of customer expectations, and this keeps our brand fresh and relevant. Achieving this is no easy matter and I think any brands and any type of designers face the same problem. It's easy to fall back on what you did the last time – and that builds patterns. I believe my company wants to try and break that mould. We constantly aim to innovate and stay one step ahead. Only by doing this can we achieve "brand seeding" – effectively establishing the brand's success over the long term. The Nike brand or brand experience is based on sowing the seed of a memory in your customer's mind, so that you can draw on that memory again – "harvest" it – weeks, months, years or even decades later. Our NikeTown programmes have been very successful in getting customers to come back to the space, because the space changes constantly. It keeps itself fresh and vibrant. And in renewing the space, we offer new products, new messages, new communications.

_____Otto Riewoldt: New shopping centres need their own brand character, too. They have to be designed so as to attract the public on their own account, while at the same time functioning effectively as catwalks for the brands on display. How have the architects at RKW faced up to this challenge?

Workshop-Diskussion

Teilnehmer: John Hoke, Global Image Design, Nike, Beaverton, USA, Massimo Iosa Ghini, Architekt und Designer, Bologna, Jens Kalkbrenner, Architekt, ECE Hamburg, Johannes Ringel, Architekt, RKW, Architekten Düsseldorf

Moderation: Burkhard Fröhlich, Chefredakteur DBZ, Gütersloh, Otto Riewoldt, Architekturjournalist, Köln

---

_____Burkhard Fröhlich: Wenn es um Brandscaping, um das dreidimensionale Gestalten von Markenlandschaften geht, was sind die besten Ansätze für neue Wege, zum Beispiel aus Sicht der Weltmarke Nike?

_____John Hoke: Für uns ist es das Wichtigste, dass wir den Kundenkontext genau verstehen, bevor wir ein Projekt realisieren. Dann versuchen wir, eine Vision zu schaffen, die dem Kunden als Leitfaden dient, die für ihn relevant ist und auf Widerhall stößt. Viele unserer Designlösungen sind also vorausschauend, damit unsere Marke immer ihre Frische bewahrt. Das ist sicher ganz schön schwierig, und dieses Problem haben im Grunde alle Marken und alle Gestalter. Es ist viel einfacher, auf Altbewährtes zurückzugreifen und eine Routine zu entwickeln. Wir bei Nike aber tun alles, um lebendig zu bleiben. Wir wollen immer innovativ einen Schritt voraus sein. Nur so können wir langfristig das, was wir Brand-Seeding nennen, das dauerhafte „Einsäen" des Markenimages erreichen. Das mit der Gestaltung verbundene Markenerlebnis muss dem Besucher so klar ins Gedächtnis gebrannt werden, dass man die Erinnerung noch Wochen, Monate, Jahre und Jahrzehnte später abrufen und sich entsprechend zunutze machen kann. Mit den NikeTown-Konzepten haben wir das geschafft, weil diese Orte vor Leben sprudeln und sich ständig selbst erneuern – mit neuen Aktivitäten, ständig neuen Produkten, neuen Botschaften und den neuesten Nachrichten.

_____Otto Riewoldt: Wenn neue Einkaufszentren geplant werden, müssen auch solche Orte eigenen Markencharakter mit hoher Popularität ausbilden und zugleich als optimaler Laufsteg für die dort angebotenen Marken fungieren. Hier liegt ein Schwerpunkt der Planungsarbeit der Architekten von RKW.

Burkhard Fröhlich

Massimo Iosa Ghini

Johannes Ringel

_____Johannes Ringel: Uns beschäftigt aktuell als Thema die Renaissance des Warenhauses im „neuen Look", die Aufwertung von innerstädtischen Liegenschaften zu neuen City-Malls. Leitmotive sind: ein lebendiges Gebäude, großzügig, gut ausgeleuchtet, leicht, gut belüftet, transparent. Wir wollen uns ganz bewusst wieder um den Kunden bemühen und dabei gleichzeitig eine Bühne schaffen, um zu sehen und gesehen zu werden, auf der Kunden und Einzelhändler interagieren können und die dem veränderten Verbraucherverhalten gerecht wird, ein Gebäude, das in einem urbanen Kontext Meilensteine und Akzente setzt.

_____Burkhard Fröhlich: In welche Richtung hat sich das Verbraucherverhalten denn verändert?

_____Johannes Ringel: Alle Wettbewerber, alle Marken fragen sich: Was zieht die Leute an? Was bringt sie dazu, in die Stadt zu gehen? Meist ist es doch so, dass die Leute deshalb in die City strömen, weil sie Abwechslung und Unterhaltung haben wollen. Die Kunden suchen Spaß und Zerstreuung beim Einkaufserlebnis.

_____Massimo Iosa Ghini: Ich stimme Ihnen zu, bin mir allerdings nicht ganz sicher, ob wir im Design von Verkaufsflächen tatsächlich nur den Endverbraucher im Sinn haben. Mein Kunde ist das beauftragende Unternehmen und das wichtigste Ziel liegt darin, sicherzustellen, dass sich das jeweilige Produkt von anderen unterscheidet und dass diese Differenzierung auch sichtbar gemacht wird. Ich weiß, wovon ich spreche, denn wir gestalten beides: Produkte und Shops. Worauf es ankommt, ist, durch unterschiedliche Eigenschaften diesen Unterschied deutlich zu machen. Das ist unser Job.

_____Burkhard Fröhlich: Ihr Studio hat für Marken verschiedenster Branchen Shops und POS-Designs entwickelt. Welche Rolle spielt die Gestaltung als Imageträger?

_____Massimo Iosa Ghini: Image ist längst nicht mehr alles, das Leben besteht aus vielen verschiedenen Elementen. Deshalb geht es heute darum, im Brandscaping andere Wege zu finden, um das Produkt in das Zentrum des Interesses zu rücken. Mein Freund Ettore Sottsass hat einmal gesagt, dass wir wie Sänger sind. Jeder singt sein Lied und jeder will ganz vorne auf der Bühne stehen. Unsere Tätigkeit berührt die Architektur ebenso wie das Design und die Kommunikation. Wir müssen die Unternehmensphilosophie herausarbeiten, und diese Entwicklungsstufen laufen ab vor der eigentlichen Gestaltungsaufgabe für die Shops. Das setzt bereits bei der Corporate Identity an. Für viele Kunden haben wir daher eine Design Identity entwickelt als jene Unterneh-

_____Johannes Ringel: A crucial issue for us at present is the renaissance of the department store. These city-centre properties are being given a new look – the defaults being a vibrant atmosphere, a feeling of spaciousness, good lighting, fresh air and transparency. Our primary point of reference is the customer – our aim is to create a stage on which to see and be seen, a stage where customers and retailers can interact, responding to new trends in customer behaviour and defining the parameters for a new urban style.

_____Burkhard Fröhlich: In what direction is consumer behaviour shifting?

_____Johannes Ringel: What everyone's asking is: what attracts people? What gives them a reason to go into town? And generally the answer is that they are looking for fun and entertainment – which is what they want from their retail experience, too.

_____Massimo Iosa Ghini: I agree with you, but I am not sure that we are working for the end customer when we design retail outlets. Personally, I feel that my client is the company. The main aim is to set that company apart from the competition and to make this difference visible.

Otto Riewoldt   John Hoke   Jens Kalkbrenner

mensaussage, die gleich nach der Corporate Identity kommt, also das Logo, die Marke. Das heißt, dass in solchen Fällen die Identität entweder erneuert oder ganz neu geschaffen werden musste und dann an die Kunden und an den Einzelhandel kommuniziert wurde.

_____Otto Riewoldt: Neue Identität für alte Nutzungen könnte auch das Motto sein für die Umwidmung von großen historischen Bahnhofskomplexen in florierende Einkaufspassagen. Die Entwicklungs- und Betreibergesellschaft ECE ist diesen Weg gegangen in verschiedenen deutschen Großstädten. Wird hier demonstriert, was der Architekturvordenker Rem Koolhaas meint, wenn er sagt: „Das Einkaufen kann jeden anderen Aspekt des urbanen Lebens kolonialisieren, wenn nicht sogar ersetzen…"?

_____Jens Kalkbrenner: Eigentlich schon. Anfangs stießen wir auf sehr großen Widerstand. Die Angst ging um, dass durch diese Kommerzialisierung die historischen Bahnhöfe in ihrer Substanz zerstört werden könnten. Es gab viele kritische Stimmen, die sagten: „Was soll dieser gigantische Konsumtempel hier? Sie verderben doch nur den Läden in der Innenstadt das Geschäft". Und was geschah? Genau das Gegenteil. Die Leute beginnen in Leipzig zum Beispiel ihren Einkaufsbummel am Hauptbahnhof und gehen von hier aus weiter in die City. Leipzig war wie Köln oder Hannover ein Pilotprojekt, bei dem wir versucht haben, die Bahnhofsphilosophie mit der Einkaufsphilosophie zu verbinden. Dabei half unsere Erfahrung, um das jeweilige Projekt mit dem richtigen Branchenmix als Produkt zu definieren und zu platzieren. Natürlich muss auch noch eine Portion Experimentierfreudigkeit hinzukommen. Und der Erfolg gibt uns recht: Selbst Markenunternehmen, die bei den ersten Sondierungsgesprächen noch ablehnend waren, sind heute unter den Mietern oder Interessenten, denn es hat sich gezeigt, dass die Umsätze dort hundertprozentig stimmen. Sie sehen die Mischung, und sie sehen auch, dass hier etwas Neues gelungen ist, und zwar allen Unkenrufen zum Trotz.

_____Johannes Ringel: Bei Anbietern wie Nike zeigt sich, dass man versucht, die Topmarken direkt beim Endverbraucher zu vermarkten, statt wie üblich über die Einzelhandelsschiene. Wird sich dieser Trend verstärken oder durchsetzen, kann und soll man die traditionellen Absatzmittler umgehen?

_____John Hoke: Ich glaube, das wird sich immer mehr durchsetzen, weil man so die Reinheit der Marke, das pure Markenverständnis direkt gegenüber dem Kunden kommunizieren kann. Die Leute suchen im Einzelhandel nach einem überzeugenden Markenausdruck, der ihnen den Weg weist. Sie kaufen nicht nur ein Produkt, sondern die Ethik und

I say this as someone who operates on both sides of the fence, as it were: I design shops, but I also design products. The ultimate goal is to create this difference, drawing on a variety of resources. That's how I see our job.

_____Burkhard Fröhlich: Your studio has designed shops and developed POS designs for brands in a wide range of fields. What do you see as the role of design in creating and conveying an image?

_____Massimo Iosa Ghini: Nowadays, image is no longer top of the list of priorities: life is composed of so many different elements. Brandscaping today is more a question of finding new ways of placing the product on centre-stage. My friend Ettore Sottsass once said, "We are like singers, everybody sings his song and we all want to be in the spotlight". Our work concerns architecture as much as design and communications. We have to convey and express the company's philosophy. First we must define what this philosophy involves before we can move on to design the retail space itself. Corporate identity is the starting point. For many of our clients we have developed a design identity devolved directly from their corporate identity, that is to say the logo, the brand. Ultimately, it was a question of renewing or completely

redesigning the identity and then communicating it to customers and retailers.

_____Otto Riewoldt: "New identity for old" could also be the motto for the conversion of large-scale, historical railway station complexes into flourishing shopping malls – the type of project undertaken by developer and operating company ECE in a number of major German cities. Do such projects perhaps reveal what avant-garde architect Rem Koolhaas meant when he said "Shopping can colonize, or even replace, every other aspect of urban life...?"

_____Jens Kalkbrenner: In a sense, yes. In the beginning we met with considerable resistance. People were worried that we might destroy the historical fabric of the stations by converting them for commercial use. Our many critics protested that by establishing these major retail projects we would take business away from the city-centre stores. And what happened? Exactly the opposite. In Leipzig, for example, people start their shopping spree at the station complex and move on from there to the city centre. Leipzig, like Cologne and Hanover, was a pilot project, where we were seeking to combine the original ethos of the railway station with the spirit of today's retail world. Here our experience was a great help in defining and positioning each project as a product, with the right mix of retail outlets within the shopping centre. Of course there is always an element of spontaneity or experiment. And the outcome has proven us right: even brands that had reservations in the initial stages are now among our tenants or prospective tenants, because the sales figures show that we've hit the nail on the head. They see the mix and they also see that we've succeeded in creating something new and different – whatever the critics may have said at the outset.

_____Johannes Ringel: With major brands like Nike there is a trend towards marketing the top brands directly to the end consumer, bypassing the traditional "middle man". Do you think that this trend is set to continue?

_____John Hoke: I think so, yes. What is interesting about direct retail is that you are able to communicate the purity, the pure understanding of the brand directly to the consumer. When people walk into a shopping location they are not just buying the product, they are also buying into the ethic of the company – this is what they really care about. In the past this aspect has been somewhat neglected or devalued. Nike and a few other brands have decided that it is an important message. Our NikeTown programme is really more like a three-dimensional advert. We see it as our company's highest form of expression.

letztlich die Seele des Unternehmens. Dieser Aspekt ist in der Vergangenheit etwas vernachlässigt worden. Nike und einige andere Marken haben beschlossen, dass dies anders werden soll. Unser NikeTown-Programm ist eigentlich eine dreidimensionale Werbung. Es ist für uns die höchste Ausdrucksform unseres Unternehmens. Sie erleben Nike-Town live statt nur auf einem Bildschirm. Das macht einen Großteil des Erfolgs dieses speziellen Konzepts aus.

_____Burkhard Fröhlich: Aber Sie agieren im Direktverkauf auch mit den weniger aufwändigen Nike Outlets. Haben Sie Pläne, noch weiter zu segmentieren?

_____John Hoke: Ja, die haben wir. Die NikeTowns sind so groß, dass sie Touristenattraktionen bilden. Natürlich ist es super, als Marke ein richtiger Publikumsmagnet zu sein. Die Zukunft liegt aber auch in kleineren, auf einzelne Zielgruppen bezogenen Einheiten. Neben den megagroßen Stores, die die Massen anziehen, richten wir zurzeit eine ganze Reihe von Shops ausschließlich mit Sportbekleidung für Frauen ein. Es gibt noch weitere Vorhaben: ein Kids-Konzept, Pläne für reine Sportschuhgeschäfte.

_____Otto Riewoldt: Was hat der Einzelhandel inzwischen von der Unterhaltungsbranche gelernt?

_____Massimo Iosa Ghini: Heute gibt es handfeste Verbindungen zwischen der Unterhaltungsbranche und dem Handel. Aus Kundengesprächen weiß ich, dass es vor allem um das Einkaufserlebnis, um die unvergessliche Einkaufserfahrung geht. Natürlich betritt man ein Geschäft, um etwas zu kaufen, aber den tatsächlichen Raum betritt man, weil man auf der Suche nach einem Erlebnis ist. Ich glaube, dass sich hier zur Zeit einiges verändert. John Hoke hat völlig recht, wenn er sagt, dass ein Shop nicht primär eine Einkaufsquelle ist, sondern ein Ort, an dem man den Unternehmensgeist erleben und verstehen kann. Ich habe die Vision, dass der Shop der Zukunft wie eine Art Disneyland sein könnte, natürlich mit anderen Bildwelten und Schwerpunkten. Es könnte ein sehr spiritueller Raum sein, absolut pur, absolut organisch. Die Atmosphäre ist ganz wichtig. Das Produkt selbst ist dann nur noch ein Teil der Erfahrung, es bleibt wichtig, ist aber bei weitem nicht der Hauptakteur.

_____Johannes Ringel: Viele Besucher wollen vor allem Unterhaltung, Interaktion ist das Schlüsselwort in vielen Geschäften. Außerdem entstehen jetzt auch Themenparks, die zugleich Einkaufszentrum sind, zum Beispiel der Space Park in Bremen. Dieses Projekt wird einerseits Vergnügungspark, andererseits Einkaufszentrum sein. Zusammen wird

Our customers experience NikeTown live, not on a screen – an immediacy that accounts for much of the success of this particular concept.

_____Burkhard Fröhlich: But your direct retail operations also include the smaller-scale Nike outlets. Are you planning any other forms of segmentation?

_____John Hoke: Yes, we are. NikeTowns are so big, they are tourist attractions. And that is fantastic if you look at a tourist location opportunity, but we also believe that for a brand to speak directly to its true customers, it needs also to operate on a smaller scale. Beyond the tourist attractions we are putting up a series of women's sports stores and there are also other concepts – a kids' concept, for example, and a footwear-only concept.

_____Otto Riewoldt: What has the retail sector learned from the entertainment industry?

_____Massimo Iosa Ghini: Today, there is a real connection between the world of entertainment and the retail environment. I know from talking to customers that the most important thing about shopping is the experience. Of course you go into a shop to buy something – but you go into a space for an experience. I can see things changing here. I agree with John Hoke when he says that a shop, first and foremost, is a space where you can experience and understand the spirit of the company. My vision is that the shop of the future could be something like Disneyland – obviously adapted to different contexts, and with different images. It could be a very spiritual space, very pure, very organic. The product then becomes just one part of the experience, not the main player.

_____Johannes Ringel: Many visitors to shopping centres are looking first and foremost for entertainment. Interaction is the key element for a lot of shops. And we now have theme parks combined with shopping centres, like the Space Park in Bremen. The Space Park covers some 60,000 to 80,000 square metres and includes both entertainment facilities and a full-scale shopping centre. The theme itself was a natural choice for Bremen – the aerospace industry has a long tradition in the city – and is reflected in the design of the shopping centre, including the restaurants and cafés. Incidentally, there was no real need for such a shopping centre within Bremen, which has very good retail facilities – the aim was to attract customers from further afield.

_____Jens Kalkbrenner: The people who work in our shopping centres have to be very extrovert and enjoy selling. As architects we have al-

das Areal über eine Grundfläche von 60.000 bis 80.000 Quadratmetern verfügen. Das Ganze wirkt überhaupt nicht künstlich oder aufgesetzt, denn die Raumfahrt hat in Bremen eine lange Tradition, und so entschloss man sich, einen Freizeitpark zu diesem Thema zu bauen. Auch das Design des Einkaufszentrums steht unter dem Motto Raumfahrt bis hin zur Gastronomie. Eine Notwendigkeit, solch ein Einkaufszentrum in Bremen zu errichten, bestand übrigens nicht, denn die Versorgung mit Einzelhandelsgeschäften ist in der Stadt sehr gut. Aber man wollte Besucher und Gäste von weit her locken.

_____Jens Kalkbrenner: Die Menschen, die in unseren Einkaufszentren arbeiten, müssen vor allem extrovertiert sein und Freude am Verkaufen haben. Für die Architekten gilt es, in den Projekten Ereignisbereiche für besondere Veranstaltungen zu schaffen. Im Leipziger Hauptbahnhof spielt dann zum Beispiel ein Sinfonieorchester. So etwas unterhält die Leute. Alleiniger Zweck solcher Aktionen ist es, die Leute in das Einkaufszentrum zu ziehen. Wir lernen also sicher von der Unterhaltungsbranche.

_____Burkhard Fröhlich: Eigentlich sind die neuen Verkaufswelten schon ein Stück Unterhaltungsindustrie.

_____John Hoke: Das Stichwort heißt Retail Entertainment, Verkaufen als Unterhaltung. Wir haben uns bewusst vor zehn Jahren die verschiedensten Vergnügungstempel am Broadway angesehen, die Theater, die Kinos. Und kamen zu dem Schluss, dass es nicht mehr ausreicht, ein Produkt anzubieten. Die Leute wollen mehr, sie wollen eine Story, sie wollen Gefühle und körperlich wie emotional reagieren. In unseren Projekten geht es vor allem um Eskapismus, um die Flucht aus dem Alltag, um Fantasie und letztlich um Inspiration. Diese Zielsetzungen gehen für mich weit über die reinen Verkaufszwecke hinaus. Die Unterhaltungsbranche bietet uns solche Gefühle in Vollendung. Der Einzelhandel muss vor allem lernen, dass er mit sehr vielen anderen Dingen konkurrieren muss, die den Kunden beschäftigen. Ein Shop und ein Kino waren früher keinesfalls Wettbewerber, jetzt schon. Heute konkurrieren sie um die Zeit und das Geld der Kunden.

_____Otto Riewoldt: Ich habe hier zehn goldene Regeln, die der Disney-Konzern vor Jahrzehnten für seine Themenparks aufgestellt hat. Sie lauten: 1. Machen Sie sich mit Ihren Kunden vertraut. 2. Versetzen Sie sich in die Rolle Ihrer Kunden. Vergessen Sie nicht den menschlichen Faktor. 3. Organisieren Sie den Fluss von Ideen und Mitarbeitern. 4. Schaffen Sie einen visuellen Magneten. 5. Kommunizieren Sie in optisch verständlicher Form. 6. Vermeiden Sie Überlastungen, schaffen Sie Anmacher. 7. Machen Sie immer nur eine Sache auf einmal. 8. Ver-

ways had to incorporate areas for special events and activities into our designs. A symphony orchestra has performed in the Leipzig station complex, for example. That's the kind of entertainment people like. The sole purpose of such events is to bring people into the shopping centre. For our part, we have certainly learned from the entertainment business.

_____ Burkhard Fröhlich: You could say that these new retail environments are already part of the entertainment industry.

_____ John Hoke: The keyword is retail entertainment, selling as a form of entertainment. Ten years ago we consciously went out to other entertainment venues, the Broadway stages in New York City, the cineplexes. The general public has a sense that they want more – they want a story, they want emotions, they want to react very strongly, both physically and emotionally. With our stores the idea is about escape, about getting away from everyday life, about fantasy and ultimately about inspiration. For me these experiences transcend the goods that are sold. The entertainment business does a very nice job at that. Retailers have to learn that we are competing with many other things that take up consumers' mindspace and time. So what used to be a non-competitive landscape – a retail store and a movie never competed – is now a competitive one. The retail and entertainment worlds are competing for the customer's time and money. And it is a tough market.

_____ Otto Riewoldt: I have here the ten golden rules that Disney drew up for their theme parks ten years ago. They are: 1. Know your audience. 2. Wear your guests' shoes, i.e. don't forget the human factor. 3. Organize the flow of people and ideas. 4. Create a visual magnet. 5. Communicate with visual literacy. 6. Avoid overloads, create turn-ons. 7. Tell one story at a time. 8. Avoid contradiction, maintain identity. 9. For every ounce of treatment, provide a ton full of treats. 10. Keep it up. Basically it reads like the blueprint for today's brandscaping.

_____ Burkhard Fröhlich: I would like to hear more about designing emotions. How do you do that?

_____ Massimo Iosa Ghini: Like any other designer, I start from myself, from my background and culture. I say this because there are two schools of thought on this subject. One relies on market research findings for its answers; the other – what I call the Italian approach – proceeds quite differently: here the designers get together with the clients and talk, and gradually the aim begins to crystallize. I draw on my own visual culture and transmit this culture to a product or a space. Before

meiden Sie Widersprüche. Bewahren Sie Ihre Identität. 9. Garantieren Sie eine Tonne besonderen Genuss bei jedem Gramm Show. 10. Bleiben Sie am Ball. Im Grund genommen liest sich das wie die Vorlage für das Brandscaping von heute.

_____ Burkhard Fröhlich: Angesprochen wurde eben das Design von Emotionen, wie muss man sich das als konkrete Aufgabe vorstellen?

_____ Massimo Iosa Ghini: Ich beginne, genau wie alle anderen Designer, bei mir selbst, beginne mit meiner eigenen Kultur. Ich sage das deshalb so deutlich, weil es zu diesem Thema zwei verschiedene Schulen gibt. Die eine lässt sich alles vorschreiben von den Erkenntnissen der Marktforschung, die zweite, ich nenne sie die italienische, läuft anders ab: Man setzt sich hin, spricht miteinander und so ganz langsam kristallisiert sich dann das Ziel heraus. Ich habe eine bestimmte visuelle Kultur und diese Kultur übertrage ich auf ein Produkt oder auf einen Raum. Bevor ich tatsächlich mit der Arbeit beginne, weiß ich selbst nicht, wie die Reaktion darauf ausfallen wird. Man muss bereit sein, etwas zu riskieren, um die neuesten Trends zu beeinflussen. Man darf beim Design nicht von dem ausgehen, was derzeit auf dem Markt läuft. Vielmehr muss man Konzepte losgelöst vom Markt entwickeln. Denn der Markt ist zwar unser Ziel, aber nicht unser Ausgangspunkt.

_____ Otto Riewoldt: Steht bei dem Designprozess für diese Verkaufsumgebungen das rein Visuelle im Vordergrund oder werden auch andere Sinne angesprochen?

_____ John Hoke: Wenn wir einen neuen Shop planen, achten wir darauf, dass wir mit dem Design alle Sinne ansprechen. Wir versuchen, ihn optisch spektakulär zu gestalten, wir versuchen die Kunden durch Gerüche zu gewinnen, die bestimmte Emotionen erwecken und wir wollen, dass unsere Produkte auch haptisch durch die verwendeten Materialien inspiriert sind. Je stärker Sie die Sinne einbeziehen können, desto allumfassender ist die Gesamterfahrung. Wir haben in der Kultur, in der wir aufgewachsen sind, ein sehr visuell geprägtes Verständnis von der Welt, zunehmend beschränkt auf eine zweidimensionale Ausdrucksform, auf Computer oder Fernsehen. Ein Teil unserer Arbeit besteht darin, die Welt nicht nur virtuell, sondern real erlebbar zu machen.

_____ Burkhard Fröhlich: Welche neuen Technologien oder Materialien unterstützen die emotionale Dimension in den Einkaufsumgebungen?

I do this I don't know what the response will be. You have to be prepared to take risks if you are going to influence contemporary trends. As a designer you cannot take current market fashions as your point of departure. On the contrary, you must develop concepts independently of the market. The market may be our goal, but it is not our point of departure.

_____Otto Riewoldt: In the process of designing retail environments is the emphasis on the purely visual, or are the other senses taken into account, too?

_____John Hoke: When we are designing a new store we make sure that the design takes all the senses into account. We try to create a design that is visually spectacular, and to seduce our customers with fragrances that conjure up particular emotions; we also design our products to be attractive in tactile terms, through the materials we use. To create a total experience you have to involve all the senses. In the culture we have grown up with, our understanding of the world is a highly visual one, increasingly restricted to two-dimensional forms of expression based on a computer or a television screen. Part of our work is to convey a real experience of the world, not a virtual one.

_____Burkhard Fröhlich: What new technologies and materials can you draw on to shape the emotional dimension of retail environments?

_____John Hoke: In the past, the tools we had at our disposal were largely non-emotive ones. With today's technologies – encompassing lighting, smell, sound and vision – we are definitely able to pinpoint emotions in each customer. But there is another issue that concerns me, here. The situation in the US has become really quite extreme: we use brands to express ourselves – I'm sure the same is true in Europe, too. The brands that you select, the things you wear, the car that you drive, express who you are. The interesting thing is that traditional means of expression, such as religion and age, have become largely irrelevant. Instead the focus is on the things that you choose. This gives the design profession a very elevated status: we help determine how people express their personal feelings. Arguably a dangerous place to be in – but this is what's happening. Brands and companies are rising in stature because some of the traditional means of expression are gradually disappearing. I can't say if it's right or wrong, but that's certainly what is happening.

_____Jens Kalkbrenner: At my company we design atmosphere first and foremost – and this naturally generates and modulates emotions. Unfortunately in many of our shopping centres the stimuli we use are

_____John Hoke: Die Mittel, die uns früher zur Verfügung standen, waren auf Serviceleistungen begrenzt ohne emotionale Komponenten. Mit Technologien wie Beleuchtung, Gerüchen, Klängen und optischen Eindrücken kann man heute zweifelsohne gezielt Gefühle beim Kunden hervorrufen. Aber mich beschäftigt noch etwas anderes: In den USA sind wir inzwischen in einer schwierigen Situation. Wir nutzen bestimmte Marken dazu, um uns selbst zu definieren. Ich nehme an, in Europa hat dieser Trend ebenfalls Einzug gehalten. Die favorisierte Marke, das Modelabel, das man trägt, das Auto, das man fährt, alles ist ein Ausdruck dessen, wer und was man ist. Interessanterweise schert sich heute niemand mehr um traditionelle Kategorien wie Religion und Alter. Stattdessen werden die Produkte, die man für sich aussucht, immer wichtiger. Das bedeutet, dass der Designer eine sehr exponierte Stellung einnimmt, denn wir bestimmen mit, wie die Menschen ihre persönlichen Gefühle zum Ausdruck bringen. Ich weiß, dass das eine gefährliche Position ist, aber die Dinge entwickeln sich tatsächlich in diese Richtung. Die Marken und die dazugehörigen Unternehmen gewinnen an Statur, weil einige der traditionellen Ausdrucksformen allmählich verschwinden. Ob das nun falsch oder richtig ist, wage ich nicht zu beurteilen, es ist eben so.

_____Jens Kalkbrenner: Was mein Unternehmen angeht, so planen und entwerfen wir vor allem Atmosphäre, die natürlich Emotionen steuert. Leider arbeiten wir in zahlreichen unserer Einkaufszentren noch immer viel zu viel mit eher billigen Stimulationen, hier sehe ich durchaus Raum und Potenzial, um mit besserer Architektur und neuen Mitteln Wirkung zu erzielen.

_____Otto Riewoldt: Können auch Architekten beim Entwurf emotionaler Verkaufsräume heute mehr Risiken eingehen?

_____Johannes Ringel: Ich hätte nichts dagegen, aber da ziehen unsere Kunden nicht mit. Aber zurück zu Ihrer Frage, wie gestaltet man Emotionen? Ich glaube, dass jeder Mensch ein Gefühl für seinen eigenen Lebensstil hat beziehungsweise weiß, wie er leben möchte. Egal, ob man nun ein Produkt oder den Verkaufsraum selbst gestaltet, dieser Akt ist so etwas wie ein Spiegel für den Kunden, und wenn er sich in diesem Spiegel wiederfindet, seinen eigenen Lebensstil sieht oder das, was er sein möchte, dann fühlt er sich wohl. Erkennt er sich nicht wieder, dann fühlt er sich fremd, auch das ist Emotion.

_____Burkhard Fröhlich: Wir sind heute mit dieser Runde bei einem der führenden Lichtunternehmen zu Gast, aber nicht nur deshalb will ich fragen, ob das Gestaltungsmittel Licht für die Gestaltung von Erlebnisräumen im Handel an Bedeutung gewinnt?

still fairly crude – this is an area where I see considerable scope and potential for creating stronger emotional effects, not least through architectural means.

_____Otto Riewoldt: Should today's architects, too, be taking more risks in the design of "emotive" retail spaces?

_____Johannes Ringel: I would like to but our clients are not interested. But let me return to your question about how to design emotions. I think that every individual has an intuitive sense for their own preferred lifestyle. Designing a product or the store itself is rather like holding a mirror up to the customer. If he sees himself reflected in the mirror – if he sees his lifestyle or what he wants to be – then he feels good. Even if what he sees jars in some ways with his expectations you have still created an emotional response.

_____Burkhard Fröhlich: For today's discussion we are the guests of one of the leading lighting companies – but that's not the only reason why I want to ask whether lighting is becoming more important in the design of contemporary retail environments?

_____Jens Kalkbrenner: In my view light is part of architecture. Lighting experts should be consulted and involved in the project from a very early stage, in order to achieve the optimum solution, the optimum product.

_____Massimo Iosa Ghini: I am convinced that the material elements in space are steadily becoming less important and that attention will be focused increasingly on the immaterial and on lighting. By this I mean active lighting concepts above all – these allow you to change the atmosphere of a space whatever the time of day, varying the mood and effect. Another key aspect here is the incorporation of screens and projections into architecture. I think this will become more and more prevalent: effectively screens are a light source that can be used to convey information, present images and create special effects.

_____Johannes Ringel: For me lighting ranks among the five most important elements in shop design and architecture. Good lighting is essential for effective product presentation, especially if retailers are moving back into the city centres, where the lighting conditions in old buildings are often far from ideal. The aim, of course, is to create a bright, well-illuminated environment – but not all architects realize that it is worth investing heavily in lighting design. There is still a lack of awareness about the possibilities here.

_____Jens Kalkbrenner: Für mich ist Licht ein Teil der Architektur. Beleuchtungsexperten sollten bereits sehr früh beratend in das Projekt eingebunden werden, um zu einer optimalen Lösung, zu einem optimalen Produkt zu gelangen.

_____Massimo Iosa Ghini: Ich bin überzeugt, dass das Materielle im Raum immer mehr in den Hintergrund rückt und dass stattdessen das Immaterielle, auch das Licht, immer wichtiger wird. Damit meine ich insbesondere aktive Beleuchtungskonzepte, denn damit lässt sich die Atmosphäre in einem Raum unabhängig von der Tageszeit immer wieder verändern, um wechselnde Erfahrungen zu vermitteln, auch durch Veränderungen im Tagesverlauf. Der zweite wesentliche Aspekt ist die Integration von Leinwänden, Bildschirmen, Projektionen in die Architektur. Darin könnte vielleicht die Zukunft liegen, denn im Grunde handelt es sich um eine Lichtquelle, die aber Informationen vermitteln, Bilder übertragen und spezielle Effekte erzielen kann.

_____Johannes Ringel: Für mich gehört die Beleuchtung zu den fünf wichtigsten Elementen im Shop-Design und in der Architektur. Für die Präsentation der Produkte ist gute Beleuchtung unverzichtbar, insbesondere, wenn sich die Innenstädte verändern sollen und die Läden in historische Gebäude einziehen, wo man oft mit Lichtverhältnissen konfrontiert ist, die alles andere als optimal sind. Helligkeit zu schaffen, ist natürlich eine Aufgabe, aber nicht jeder Architekt sieht schon ein, dass es sich lohnt, viel Aufwand mit der Lichtgestaltung zu betreiben. Das Bewusstsein muss sich erst entwickeln.

_____Otto Riewoldt: Bei den neuen Verkaufslandschaften lassen sich im Sinne von Brandscaping zwei grundsätzlich unterschiedliche Ansätze beobachten. Der erste Ansatz läuft darauf hinaus, dass man das Geschäft als einen Raum ansieht, in dem Objekte und nicht etwa Waren ausgestellt werden, also vergleichbar mit einer musealen Galerie, während der andere das Interieur eher als Theater, als Bühnenspektakel, versteht. Beispiele für die edle, sogar mit echter Kunst geadelte Leere sind die New Yorker Flagshipstores von Armani oder Helmut Lang. Den krassen Gegensatz dazu markieren für mich beispielsweise die narrativ aufgeladenen Shopping Malls in England, wie Trafford Center in Manchester, das sowohl von außen als auch von innen wie ein Märchenschloss daherkommt. Welche Methode setzt sich Ihrer Meinung nach eher durch: „weniger ist mehr" oder „immer größer, immer mehr"?

_____John Hoke: Ich denke, dass es in den nächsten Jahren immer mehr Läden nach Galerie-Manier geben wird. Die Auswahl an Produkten erschlägt uns fast, und der wirklich smarte Händler trifft quasi eine gekonnte Vorauswahl für den Kunden aus der Vielfalt der schönen Dinge

_____Otto Riewoldt: I see two ways of approaching the brandscaping of new retail environments. The first approach is to see the shop as exhibiting objects rather than merely displaying merchandise – like a gallery or museum. The second is to see the shop as a stage, a theatre. On one hand we have upmarket showrooms with a sparse, pared-down, almost minimalist style of presentation – like the Armani and Helmut Lang flagship stores in New York, which also exhibit real works of art. On the other hand we have shopping malls in England that take a thoroughly narrative approach: they tell a story. The Trafford Centre in Manchester looks like a palace from the outside – and on the inside, too. What do you think will prevail: the "less is more" approach or dramatic, narrative overload?

_____John Hoke: I think that the next few years will show a continuing preference for shops in the gallery format. There is so much choice in the world today that a smart shop edits for you. Editing will be an important part of store merchandising, editing things from the world and presenting them as a collection. Rather than displaying everything, the buyers will take selected products and give them elevated status. I think the trend will be toward selectivity rather than overload.

_____Johannes Ringel: It depends entirely on what you want to sell and who you want to sell it to. That's what determines the choice between a gallery and a theatre. If I want to sell Guinness then I have to design an Irish pub not a gallery. That's shop design. But shop design and architecture are two very different things. Architecture looks at the broader context. Whether a shopping centre should look like a palace from the outside or not is an architectural question. And it should be the architects' responsibility, too, to ensure that a new shopping centre fits in with its urban architectural context.

_____John Hoke: We distinguish between certain corporate constants or "global equities" which are valid in all regions – our logo, for example – and the store design, where we do try to enter into the regional culture and understand the flavour of the local retail world. An example here would be the way preferences vary regarding the material we use for floor coverings. In the US we put a highly polished concrete floor in the stores and everybody thought it looked beautiful. So we decided to use the same material in Asia. However, we learned subsequently that concrete has quite different connotations in Asia, where it is widely associated with prisons. In this case we had completely misunderstood the material's regional implications. So we take great care to enter into the culture and try to understand the cultural differences, in order to present the company to optimum effect. The experience offered by NikeTown in New York is very different from that in London, in terms of

auf dieser Welt. Statt einfach alles zu zeigen, wählen die Einkäufer gezielt einige Produkte wie Objekte heraus und heben diese dadurch auf eine höhere Ebene. Ich persönlich sehe eher in dieser Entwicklung die Zukunft, als in der „immer größer, immer mehr"-Philosophie.

_____Johannes Ringel: Es kommt ganz darauf an, was man verkaufen will und wer die Zielklientel ist. Diese Frage bestimmt die Entscheidung zwischen Galerie und Theater. Wenn ich Guinness Bier verkaufen will, muss ich ein irisches Pub entwerfen und keine Galerie. So funktioniert Shop-Design, aber Shop-Design und Architektur sind zwei ganz verschiedene Dinge. Die Architektur widmet sich dem größeren Rahmen. Es ist eine Frage der Architektur, sich dafür oder dagegen zu entscheiden, dass ein Einkaufszentrum von außen wie ein Schloss aussehen soll. Und es sollte Sache der Architekten sein, die Entstehung eines Einkaufszentrums zu verhindern, das von seiner Architektur her nicht in ein Stadtbild passt.

_____John Hoke: Wir unterscheiden bestimmte Unternehmenskonstanten wie unser Logo, die wir „Global Equities" nennen und die in allen Vertriebsregionen gelten, von der Shop-Gestaltung, bei der wir anstreben, die regionale Kultur im allgemeinen und die regionale Einkaufskultur im Besonderen zu berücksichtigen. Dazu gehört beispielsweise, dass die Kunden je nach Region und Land unterschiedliche Materialien bei der Innenarchitektur bevorzugen. In den USA hatten wir zum Beispiel sehr erfolgreich einen polierten Betonfußboden verwendet, das gleiche Material setzten wir daher auch in einem unserer Shops in Asien ein. Leider erfuhren wir erst zu spät, dass bei den Asiaten Betonböden immer mit Gefängnissen assoziiert werden. In diesem Fall hatten wir die regionalen Implikationen des Materials, die damit verbundenen Assoziationen völlig missverstanden. Wir versuchen also möglichst immer die kulturellen Besonderheiten zu berücksichtigen und zu verstehen, so dass sich unser Unternehmen in jedem Markt optimal präsentieren kann. Was NikeTown in New York an Raumerlebnissen vermittelt, unterscheidet sich in den Themen, Zitaten oder Requisiten von London oder demnächst von Tokio. Es ist NikeTown mit den Augen der jeweiligen Stadt oder Kultur gesehen. Diese Vielfalt gehört zum Markenausdruck.

_____Burkhard Fröhlich: Architekten haben heute bei der Programmierung von Einkaufszentren damit zu kämpfen, dass sie es einerseits mit starken Marken, entweder Produkt- oder Shop-Marken, zu tun haben und dass es andererseits aber gilt, alle diese Marken in einem Kontext unterzubringen, der wiederum für sich selbst eine eigene unverwechselbare Identität aufbauen muss. In der Vergangenheit war

themes, quotations and props – and Tokyo will be different again. In each case it is NikeTown seen through the eyes of a particular town or culture. This diversity is part of brand expression.

_____Burkhard Fröhlich: Architects today also play a role in the programming of retail malls. The problem they face is that they have strong brands, either products or retail brands on the one hand, and the context – the mall – on the other, which has to establish its own identity against such a strong and varied backdrop. In the past it has often been a problem convincing strong brands to fit in with the larger general setting.

_____Johannes Ringel: Things have changed considerably. We have moved away from centres with standardized shop fronts and branding, which offered no scope for individual expression. Today, retailers are given a lot of freedom to develop their own concept – which is essential, given that tenancies can sometimes change hands within a very short space of time. We assume that the stores will need to be redesigned every five to eight years. In order to ensure the long-term economic viability of the building we have to make it flexible and adaptable to different trends. If the building is developed in this way from the outset, there will be no problems in the future.

_____Jens Kalkbrenner: The term of contracts with our tenants is between five and ten years. After ten years we start changing things. The products on offer, or the product philosophy, may change, and so the architecture has to keep changing, too. As regards the design of shop façades we have recently moved away from giving tenants complete freedom to design their own façades. This often leaves us at odds with the designers of individual stores, at which point we set up a constructive dialogue to find a solution. In Leipzig, for example, the conservation authorities had a good deal of influence on the development of the station buildings (as they did in other cities) but we were able to find a satisfactory solution. Naturally enough, the heritage people have a different agenda: they want pillars to remain visible, they want the façade to be historically appropriate. And so compromises have to be reached. But the new architecture in Leipzig has its own identity. This identity is so strong, without being intrusive or oppressive, that tenants, too, feel they have plenty of scope to express themselves.

_____Johannes Ringel: The secret lies in finding a 'passe-partout' – a setting that shows all the individual pictures to best effect.

_____Otto Riewoldt: I would like to come back to the problem of standardization. On the one hand we are seeing the development of stan-

das ein stetes Konfliktfeld, wenn es darum ging, Einzelmarken dazu zu bringen, sich einem größeren Rahmen anzupassen.

_____Johannes Ringel: Da hat sich inzwischen sehr viel getan. Der Trend geht weg von der einheitlichen inneren Fassade für alle Geschäfte hin zu weitgehender Gestaltungsfreiheit. Das ist auch nötig, denn die Mieter wechseln teilweise rasch. Wir gehen davon aus, dass ein Konzept eine Lebensdauer von fünf bis acht Jahren hat. Um zu gewährleisten, dass das Gebäude langfristig wirtschaftlich rentabel bleibt, muss das Shop-Design in diesen Abständen geändert werden. Das setzt voraus, dass die Architektur flexibel ist und sich den veränderten Anforderungen und Trends anpassen lässt. Wenn gleich von Anfang an so geplant wird, wird es auch in Zukunft keine Probleme geben.

_____Jens Kalkbrenner: Wir haben mit unseren Mietern Verträge mit einer Laufzeit zwischen fünf und zehn Jahren. Nach einem Jahrzehnt allerdings ist es Zeit für neue Gesichter. Manchmal ändert sich auch das Profil, die Philosophie der dort verkauften Produkte. Für solche Fälle muss auch die Architektur bereit sein, flexibel zu reagieren. Was die Gestaltung der Ladenfassaden betrifft, rücken wir in letzter Zeit wieder ab von zu weitgehenden Freiheiten. Wir liegen dabei immer wieder im Clinch mit den Innenarchitekten der einzelnen Geschäfte und versuchen den konstruktiven Dialog. In Leipzig, wo wie bei den anderen Bahnhöfen der Denkmalschutz ein gewichtiges Wort mitzureden hatte, haben wir eine gute Lösung gefunden. Für die Denkmalschutzbehörden gelten natürlich ganz andere Spielregeln. Sie wollen, dass alte Säulen sichtbar bleiben, dass die Fassade stimmig ist. Folglich müssen Kompromisse eingegangen werden. Aber die neue Architektur in Leipzig hat ihre eigene Identität. Diese ist so stark, dass auch die Mieter das Gefühl haben, dass sie sich ein gutes Stück durchsetzen konnten und die Architektur nicht störend oder aufdringlich wirkt.

_____Johannes Ringel: Das Geheimnis liegt darin, ein Passepartout zu finden, in das sich jedes einzelne Bild harmonisch einfügt und das die einzelnen Bilder optimal zur Geltung bringt.

_____Otto Riewoldt: Ich würde gerne noch einmal das Problem der Standardisierung ansprechen. Für Filialbetriebe werden Systeme entwickelt passend für alle Läden, andererseits soll doch jedes Geschäft auch einzigartig wirken. Ist das nicht ein gewisser Widerspruch?

_____Massimo Iosa Ghini: Es ist ein Trugschluss zu glauben, dass jedes Geschäft einzigartig sein muss. Das ist gar nicht so wichtig. Ein System muss im richtigen Kontext wirken und den Markenausdruck transportieren. Die Wiedererkennbarkeit ist Teil der Design-Identität.

dardized store formats – and on the other there are strong tendencies to make each shop unique. Isn't this a contradiction?

_____Massimo Iosa Ghini: I don't think every space has to be unique. That is not so important. What matters is that brand identity must be translated effectively into each individual context. The recognition factor is a key component of design identity.

_____Burkhard Fröhlich: Greenfield shopping centres are going out of fashion, and retailers and consumers are moving back into the city centres. What are the reasons behind this trend?

_____Jens Kalkbrenner: This is primarily a reaction on the part of consumers. But it is also a reaction to initiatives taken by civic authorities. They no longer want greenfield shopping centres – they want thriving city centres.

_____Otto Riewoldt: Does the same hold true in the USA, where this trend is also apparent? There, too, the high streets are coming to life again – a phenomenon that has been referred to as the "Main Street Revival". Even new shopping districts are being designed in line with traditional shopping street models.

_____John Hoke: On our part it was a conscious decision to return to the cities, to the urban culture and the heart of city life. The people are there, the infrastructure is there. The trend for moving out of the city to the suburbs is virtually being reversed now. People are now living outside the cities, and the cities act as a cultural magnet. There's much more to do there – you can go downtown and see a show or shop; this is where today's themed stores belong. This seemed like a natural opportunity to go back into city centres, to help rebuild them and make them vibrant.

_____Johannes Ringel: In Germany, the move to get the retail trade back into the city is politically motivated – in economical and ecological terms it makes no sense at all to have retail facilities located out of town. Our cities had become empty and boring and the atmosphere in the shopping centres outside the cities was very artificial. They were trying to create façades like those in the historical city centres – while at the same the shops in the city itself were standing empty: a ridiculous situation. The entertainment you have to create from scratch in a greenfield shopping centre is already there for the taking in the town centres. Leipzig is the living proof that this works. In political terms the decision to have ECE bring the railway station to life with a shopping centre was perfectly judged.

_____Burkhard Fröhlich: Einkaufen auf der grünen Wiese ist passé. Es drängt den Handel und die Konsumenten wieder in die Innenstadt. Warum eigentlich?

_____Jens Kalkbrenner: Diese Entwicklung ist primär eine Reaktion der Verbraucher. Es ist aber auch eine Reaktion auf Entscheidungen der kommunalen Ebene. Die Städte wollen diese Einkaufszentren auf der grünen Wiese nicht mehr, sie setzen auf die Aufwertung lebendiger Innenstädte.

_____Otto Riewoldt: In den USA, wo dieser Trend ebenfalls zu beobachten ist, muss das aber andere Gründe haben. Auch dort beleben sich die Hauptstraßen wieder, man spricht von einem Main Street Revival. Selbst neue Einkaufszonen werden nach dem Muster historischer Stadtstraßen gebaut.

_____John Hoke: Wir haben uns ganz bewusst entschieden, zurück in den Stadtkern zu gehen, in die urbane Kultur zurückzukehren, weil dort das städtische Leben pulsiert. Dort haben wir das Publikum und die Infrastruktur. Der Trend, dass die Einkaufszonen an die Peripherie abwanderten, hat sich inzwischen praktisch umgekehrt. Heute leben die Leute außerhalb der City und die Städte fungieren als kultureller Magnet. Dort wartet Unterhaltung verschiedenster Art, dazu gehören heute auch die Themen-Shops in der City. Das ist unser Beitrag zur größeren städtischen Angebotsvielfalt in Sachen Freizeit.

_____Johannes Ringel: Die Entscheidung, den Einzelhandel wieder in die Innenstädte zurückzuholen, ist in Deutschland primär politisch begründet. Es macht nämlich weder ökonomisch noch ökologisch Sinn, den Einzelhandel außerhalb des Stadtkerns anzusiedeln. Unsere Städte wurden immer leerer und langweiliger und die Atmosphäre in den Einkaufszentren vor den Toren der Stadt war ausgesprochen künstlich. Es entstand die paradoxe Situation, dass man in den Vorstädten versuchte, die Fassaden der historischen Innenstadt mit architektonischen Mitteln nachzuempfinden, während der echte Stadtkern darnieder lag und hinter den Schaufensterfassaden gähnende Leere herrschte. Dabei steht doch alles, was man zur Unterhaltung braucht, sozusagen griffbereit im Stadtzentrum. Die Unterhaltungsmöglichkeiten, die in einem Einkaufszentrum erst künstlich geschaffen werden müssen, sind in der Innenstadt schon zur Verfügung. Dass es funktioniert, zeigt das Beispiel Leipzig. Politisch gesehen, war die Entscheidung, ECE mit diesem großen Einkaufszentrum im Bahnhof nach Leipzig zu bringen, genau richtig.

_____Burkhard Fröhlich: What about the CentrO project in Oberhausen, where a disused industrial site has been transformed into an artificial "shopping city". Isn't that dragging the old town centre into a downward spiral?

_____Johannes Ringel: In this case it was a question of developing a new urban vision after the collapse of the coal and steel industries. The whole point was that the town did not have what you might call a traditional centre. So, if its cohesion was to be maintained when the industries to which it owed its existence failed, a new city centre had to be created. And the ideal location was right in the middle of the three former villages that were once combined to make up the original Oberhausen. The aim was to create the best and most popular shopping city in the region and it worked. In addition to the shopping centre, the project includes a multi-purpose arena as well as pleasant, affordable apartments and houses. Now the areas between CentrO and the surrounding parts of Oberhausen are gradually being filled in with office buildings and private housing. The best news of all is that a science park is planned – incorporating five Fraunhofer institutes along with other facilities, including a hotel. So the shopping centre was definitely a catalyst for achieving local government's aim of high-quality urban development.

_____Otto Riewoldt: We cannot discuss changes in brand strategies and marketing without mentioning the new electronic media. In what ways is e-commerce influencing the character and design of retail spaces? Is this new source of competition another reason to enhance the retail experience, emphasising the attraction of the real over the virtual?

_____Johannes Ringel: The Internet is just one medium, it doesn't exclude the others. You may have a telephone – but you still meet people face to face. We have televisions – but television didn't bring about the downfall of cinemas and theatres. We may have the virtual office – but we still need real office buildings where we can communicate directly with each other. When it comes to shopping, there is no substitute for the immediate tactile experience of picking up the object you wish to buy.

_____Burkhard Fröhlich: Does e-commerce represent a significant market for companies such as Nike?

_____John Hoke: We have undertaken some experimental projects on the Internet, but for our brand this is not really an effective distribution channel. When you're buying a shoe you want to try it on, see how it feels and how it looks – an experience that's simply not possible on the Internet.

_____Burkhard Fröhlich: Was aber ist mit dem CentrO-Projekt in Oberhausen, wo eine Industriebrache zur künstlichen Einkaufsstadt wurde und das alte städtische Zentrum kommerziell ausblutet?

_____Johannes Ringel: Hier musste man nach dem Zusammenbruch von Kohle und Stahl eine neue urbane Vision entwickeln, um den nur durch die Schwerindustrie geschaffenen Zusammenhalt der Stadt zu sichern. Nach dem Motto, „Wir haben keinen Stadtkern, also müssen wir ein neues Stadtzentrum schaffen", entschied man sich dafür, genau in der geographischen Mitte zwischen den drei ehemaligen Dörfern, aus denen das alte Oberhausen bestand, die „neue Mitte" zu bauen. Der Gedanke war, die beste und beliebteste Einkaufsstadt Nordrhein-Westfalens zu werden, und man hat es geschafft. Nicht nur das Einkaufszentrum, auch eine große Veranstaltungshalle und inzwischen viele bezahlbare, ansprechende Wohnungen und Häuser. Man kann beobachten, dass der Zwischenraum, der das CentrO von dem umliegenden Stadtgebiet trennte, sich allmählich mit Bürogebäuden und Privathäusern füllt. Das Beste aber ist, dass jetzt auf den noch freien Flächen ein Science Park entstehen wird. Fünf Institute des Fraunhofer-Instituts und weitere Einrichtungen, auch ein Hotel, werden sich hier ansiedeln. Die Kommune hat auf diese Weise mit der Initialzündung Shopping-Center ihre Intention einer qualitativ anspruchsvollen Stadtentwicklung unbedingt erreicht.

_____Otto Riewoldt: Über Veränderungen in Markenstrategien und Vermarktungsformen kann man nicht reden, ohne die neuen elektronischen Möglichkeiten zu diskutieren. Wie beeinflusst der Internet-Handel den Charakter und das Design von Verkaufsbereichen? Liegt in der frisch gebackenen Konkurrenz auch ein Grund, das Shopping verstärkt zum Erlebnis zu machen, den Reiz der wirklichen Dinge zu betonen und statt Anklicken wahre Wunder zum Anfassen zu bieten?

_____Johannes Ringel: Das Internet ist ja nur ein neues Medium und schließt die anderen Kommunikationsformen nicht aus. Man kann viel telefonieren und trotzdem genügend persönliche Kontakte pflegen. Das Fernsehen hat Theater und Kinos nicht von der Bildfläche verdrängt. Wir haben virtuelle Büros, brauchen aber trotzdem auch reale Räume, um miteinander zu kommunizieren. Wenn wir einkaufen, ersetzt nichts das Gefühl, das Produkt als Objekt der Begierde auch in die Hand zu nehmen und zu fühlen.

_____Burkhard Fröhlich: Ist das Internet-Shopping überhaupt ein Markt für Unternehmen wie Nike?

_____Otto Riewoldt: What about the influence of interactive terminals and electronic attractions in shops?

_____John Hoke: For a while we experimented with Internet stations in our NikeTown stores because a lot of the Internet people in the company thought that this was going to be the magic formula to bring more customers into the store. Despite the fact that we had designed a nice little cover and workstation, we realised that nobody was using them. Since then we've taken all the interactive media out of the stores again, because people just aren't interested. If you're going to go out into the real world you want to speak to a real person with a pulse. When you leave home you want to be with other people – you're going from an introverted to an extroverted experience. Many of the US companies that installed computers with Internet access in their stores have since removed them.

_____Otto Riewoldt: What about technological innovations like electronic measuring booths, where you can screen yourself so that you know exactly what size you need, or booths that tell you whether the item you want is still available in your size. Levi's, for example already use systems like these in their flagship stores. Does it make sense to use these devices?

_____John Hoke: Let me tell you about the experience we had with one of our automated systems. We had a device which was based on taking off your shoe and putting your foot on a scanner. It would scan and measure your foot down to the millimetre. In fact this was one of my ideas – I felt that we could get a better fit, a better understanding of the product in this way. People were supposed to measure their left foot and their right foot together. However, as it turned out, they put their feet on separately for measurement. As a result, lots of customers were going up to the staff and asking for a right size 43 and a left size 42. If we'd carried on this way the consequences would have been catastrophic – imagine the kind of problems this would have created, from the production level onward. For a short time, Levi's used a body-measuring device, but it proved to be a complete failure with both men and women. The fact is that most people don't actually want to know their waist or hip size down to the last millimetre. The question of how much technology is going to be beneficial to the consumer, how much technology he wants and how much information is too much, certainly is an interesting one.

_____Burkhard Fröhlich: It's also revealing that companies such as Internet banks and Internet-based retailers are now seeking to consolidate their customer relationships by establishing traditional branch networks.

_____John Hoke: Wir haben versuchsweise mit dem Internet gearbeitet, doch für unsere Marke ist es nicht der geeignete Vertriebsweg. Das erste, was man tut, wenn man einen Schuh anprobiert, ist aufzustehen, um zu sehen, ob sich der Schuh bequem am Fuß anfühlt. Diese Erfahrung kann man über das Internet einfach nicht vermitteln.

_____Otto Riewoldt: Und wie sind die Erfahrungen mit interaktiven Terminals und anderen elektronischen Angeboten in den Shops?

_____John Hoke: Wir haben versuchsweise die Möglichkeit zum Surfen in unseren NikeTowns angeboten, weil viele dachten, dadurch könnte man mehr Kunden in die Geschäfte holen. Doch obwohl wir uns mit der Gestaltung sehr viel Mühe gegeben hatten, stellten wir fest, dass kein Mensch die Geräte benutzte. Also haben wir sämtliche interaktive Medien wieder abgeschafft. Wir sind sicher, dass unsere Besucher mehr Wert auf zwischenmenschliche Kontakte legen, statt nur vor so einer Kiste zu sitzen. Wer unterwegs ist, will nicht im Internet surfen, sondern sich unter echte Menschen mischen und mit ihnen kommunizieren. Das Surfen ist eine introvertierte Erfahrung, das Shoppen eine extrovertierte. Ich glaube, in den USA haben sehr viele Firmen, die in ihren Geschäften Computer mit Internetanschluss installiert hatten, die Geräte inzwischen alle wieder entfernt.

_____Otto Riewoldt: Was halten Sie von technologischen Innovationen wie elektronischen Anprobekabinen, wo elektronisch Maß genommen wird und man dann genau weiß, welche Größe man braucht, und wo man auch von der Umkleidekabine aus abfragen kann, ob ein Kleidungsstück in der gewünschten Größe verfügbar ist. Unternehmen wie Levi's arbeiten bereits in ihren Flagshipstores mit solchen Systemen. Sind solche Geräte sinnvoll?

_____John Hoke: Ich kann Ihnen gerne erzählen, wie das bei uns mit den elektronischen Fußmessgeräten ausging. Wir hatten ein Gerät entwickelt, übrigens eine von meinen Ideen, bei dem der Kunde seine Schuhe auszog und seinen Fuß auf einen Scanner stellte. Dieses Gerät vermaß den Fuß millimetergenau. Wir hatten gehofft, dass der Kunde durch dieses Gerät noch besser passende Schuhe bekommen würde. Was geschah: Die Leute vermaßen beide Füße getrennt und stellten fest, dass sie alle zwei unterschiedliche Füße hatten. Als Folge davon kamen jede Menge Kunden auf uns zu, die sagten, sie hätten gerne einen linken Schuh in Größe 42 und einen rechten in Größe 43. Wenn wir das weitergemacht hätten, hätten wir eine immense Lawine losgetreten. Stellen Sie sich vor, welche Probleme nicht nur produktionstechnischer Natur da auf uns zugekommen wären. Levi's arbeitete kurze Zeit mit einem Gerät, mit dem die Körpermaße ganz genau ge-

_____Massimo Iosa Ghini: One of our clients, Mediolanum Bank, started off as an Internet bank but realised that they also needed some showrooms in order to build a personal relationship with their clients. When it comes to finance, customers expect personal attention. They don't want to communicate exclusively with a computer screen.

_____Otto Riewoldt: Computer technologies are also opening up new possibilities for monitoring consumer behaviour in the retail environment. We are seeing the first steps towards customer tracking systems – some stores are introducing electronic devices in trolleys so that they can tell what routes customers take, how often they stop, and so on. It is no longer just about bar-coding products, it is about bar-coding customers and watching their every move, Big Brother style. Is this kind of electronic observation set to become an established feature of the brand landscape?

_____John Hoke: In our NikeTowns we have done a number of surveys with Paco Underhill, author of the book The Science of Shopping. These surveys are based on videotapes made in the store which are played in super-fast-forward mode, revealing patterns that show when customers walk in, where they stop, what they look at and where they go. They showed that when people enter a store they usually go to the right. When they see a graphic they either go towards the graphic or move away from it. However, we did not go as far as passing the information on to the design department. I believe that there are still surprises in the human being and that we don't want to pattern everything. If everything is patterned and standardized it all becomes repetitive and very dull. Sometimes I do get a little concerned that things are getting too Big Brother-ish. There is almost too much information. Personally I like to leave room for spontaneity – that's what makes life interesting, after all.

_____Burkhard Fröhlich: Could the use of such technologies be of interest for mall developers?

_____Jens Kalkbrenner: It might be but I don't think our company is going that way. We prefer to rely on our experience.

_____Burkhard Fröhlich: What do you consider the most important or exciting new development in retail design and brandscaping?

_____Massimo Iosa Ghini: The challenge is to ensure that every brandscaped space conveys the spirit of the company. This spirit is expressed through stylistic features and here it is necessary to update the style from time to time, drawing on the full range of technological

messen wurden. Das war ein totaler Flop, denn es stieß weder bei Frauen noch bei Männern auf Gegenliebe. Tatsache ist, dass die meisten Menschen ihre Taillenweite oder ihren Hüftumfang gar nicht auf den Millimeter genau wissen wollen. Deshalb hat man das Gerät dann wieder aus den Läden genommen. Die Frage, wie viel Technologie dem Kunden gut tut, wie viel Technologie er will und wo die Grenze zur Informationsüberfrachtung liegt, ist sicher sehr interessant.

_____Burkhard Fröhlich: Bezeichnend scheint auch, dass Unternehmen wie Internet-Banken und Versandhändler, die nur auf das Netz als Vertriebsweg bauten, jetzt versuchen, traditionell mit ganz realen Filialen die Kundenbindung zu stärken.

_____Massimo Iosa Ghini: Einer unserer Auftraggeber, die Bank Mediolanum, hat zunächst nur Online-Banking angeboten, dann aber erkannt, dass es trotzdem erforderlich war, einige Geschäftsräume einzurichten, damit die Kunden auch persönliche Gespräche mit Finanzberatern führen können. Wenn es um Geld geht, will der Kunde ja schließlich das Gefühl haben, dass er individuell betreut wird. Er will es nicht nur mit einem Bildschirm zu tun haben.

_____Otto Riewoldt: Neue Dimensionen eröffnet die Elektronik auch, was das Überwachen von Einkaufsgewohnheiten der Kunden angeht. Es gibt erste Versuche, das Verbraucherverhalten durch elektronisches Monitoring zum Beispiel mit entsprechend aufgerüsteten Einkaufswagen in den Geschäften zu beobachten und zu verfolgen: Welche Wege der Kunde geht und wie oft er stehen bleibt... Wer spricht heute noch vom Barcode auf dem Produkt, wenn demnächst der Kunde sozusagen mit einem Barcode versehen wird, ganz nach dem Motto: „Big Brother is watching your shopping". Wird sich das elektronische Beobachten der Kunden in der Markenlandschaft durchsetzen?

_____John Hoke: Wir haben in unseren NikeTowns bestimmte Untersuchungen mit Paco Underhill gemacht, der das Buch „The Science of Shopping" geschrieben hat. Sie basieren auf Videoaufzeichnungen in Einzelhandelsgeschäften, die im Fast-Forward-Modus abgespielt werden, so dass man die Verhaltensmuster der Kunden erkennen kann, wenn sie den Laden betreten, wo sie stehen bleiben, was sie sich ansehen und wohin sie gehen. Man hat zum Beispiel herausgefunden, dass die meisten Menschen, wenn sie in ein Geschäft kommen, zuerst nach rechts gehen. Wenn sie ein Hinweisschild sehen, lesen sie es entweder oder wenden sich ganz bewusst davon ab. Wir sind jedoch nicht so weit gegangen, dass wir diese Ergebnisse als Maßgabe an die Designabteilung weitergegeben haben. Ich glaube nämlich immer noch, dass die Menschen voller Überraschungen sind, und wir sollten

and design resources. Today's stores should appear as organic as possible, should focus on the essentials – and at the same time be distinctive and expressive.

_____Johannes Ringel: In architecture there are two main trends. First, if retailers are coming back into town, the store designs are necessarily more individualistic than in shopping centres, because they have to adapt to the existing historical buildings. Second, retailers are forging new alliances to strengthen their market position. This is a new field that will have to be developed. Ten years ago there were six or seven major department store groups in Germany, now there are only two. The vacant buildings in the city centres have yet to be redeveloped – in some cases there are 30,000 square metres standing empty. These issues will have to be tackled in the next four or five years. Hopefully such large spaces – the like of which could only be found out of town in the past – can be put to good use to help revive city-centre retailing.

_____Jens Kalkbrenner: I agree that our task for the future is to go back to historical buildings, revitalize them and liven up the city centres. At the same time we have to dedicate more time and attention to architecture, because architecture is a key factor in commercial success. And we must not be afraid of more challenging conceptual approaches here. In Berlin, for example, we collaborated with Renzo Piano, who is generally considered a very difficult partner to work with.

_____Otto Riewoldt: But success in retailing does not necessarily depend on good architecture. In Great Britain, the highest retail turnover per square metre is achieved at Heathrow Airport – no great architectural attraction. Its operators, BAA, now make more money from retail than from handling planes. Retail in fact accounts for sixty percent of their turnover.

_____Jens Kalkbrenner: We have also moved into the airport retail sector – the sales revenues it generates are phenomenal.

_____John Hoke: I think one of the biggest challenges that we face is the fact that a generation of consumers is growing up without any conception of what it means to let things mature and take effect gradually. All that counts for them is the immediate moment, the instant experience. Young kids grow up with hundreds of channels on television and the Internet gives them more information than we can ever imagine at their fingertips. So I think the challenge we face is to build physical spaces with components designed to last over time – whether this be one year, five years or 25 years – while at the same time balancing this

nicht versuchen, sie alle über einen Kamm zu scheren. Wenn alles gleich wäre und alles nach dem gleichen Muster verliefe, wäre es doch schrecklich eintönig. Manchmal mache ich mir schon Gedanken, ob die Entwicklung nicht zu sehr in Richtung „Big Brother" geht, ob nicht zu viel erforscht wird und zu viele Informationen herumschwirren. Ich wünsche mir, dass auch noch einiges der Spontaneität überlassen bleibt, denn das macht doch das Leben erst interessant.

_____Burkhard Fröhlich: Könnte der Einsatz solcher Techniken nicht gerade bei der Entwicklung von Einkaufszentren relevant sein?

_____Jens Kalkbrenner: Unter Umständen ja. Aber ich glaube nicht, dass unser Unternehmen Ambitionen in diese Richtung hat. Wir verlassen uns lieber auf unsere Erfahrung.

_____Burkhard Fröhlich: Was ist Ihrer Meinung nach die wichtigste oder interessanteste neue Entwicklung beim Brandscaping in der Einzelhandelsarchitektur?

_____Massimo Iosa Ghini: Die Herausforderung liegt darin, dass jeder als Markenlandschaft gestaltete Raum stellvertretend für den Geist des Unternehmens steht. Dieser Geist findet seinen Ausdruck in den Stilelementen und hier ist es notwendig, von Zeit zu Zeit wieder einen neuen Stil zu finden. Unter Einschluss aller technologischen und gestalterischen Möglichkeiten. Heute sollen die Läden möglichst organisch wirken. Sie sollen sich auf das Essentielle beschränken, dabei aber trotzdem Profil zeigen und expressiv sein.

_____Johannes Ringel: Im Architekturbereich gibt es zwei Trends. Erstens: Wenn die Einzelhändler wieder in die Stadt zurück kommen, muss das Shop-Design zu den historischen Gebäuden passen und deshalb individueller gestaltet werden als in einem Einkaufszentrum. Trend zwei: Die Einzelhändler gehen neue Allianzen ein, um ihre Kompetenzen zu stärken. Das ist ein neues Feld, das es zu entwickeln gilt. Nehmen Sie nur die Warenhauskonzerne, vor zehn Jahren gab es noch sechs, sieben in Deutschland, heute nur noch zwei. In den Innenstädten aber stehen die alten Liegenschaften der früheren Wettbewerber und wollen genutzt werden. Nicht selten liegen dort 30.000 Quadratmeter Fläche brach. Das sind Fragen, die in den nächsten vier oder fünf Jahren zu diskutieren sind. Es bleibt zu hoffen, dass wir Flächen dieser Größenordnung, die bis vor einigen Jahren nur außerhalb des Stadtkerns zur Verfügung standen, bald sinnvoll nützen können, damit der Handel in den Städten sich wieder belebt.

with immediacy and freshness, because that is what the consumer is going to demand. Combining this expectation of innovation with the goal of going back into the cities and converting old buildings to new uses – in my view this is the great challenge for the future. We want to remain true to our business idea and our corporate philosophy, but for brandscaping we need spaces that can be adapted quickly and flexibly to changing requirements.

The workshop "Brandscaping – New Dimensions in Retail Design" was held on 27 June, 2001 at the Zumtobel Staff Light Forum in Lemgo. It was organized by the lighting company Zumtobel Staff and the German architectural journal DBZ.

———— Jens Kalkbrenner: Ich bin auch der Ansicht, dass unsere Aufgabe für die Zukunft darin besteht, in die historische Substanz zurückzukehren, diese zu sanieren, die traditionellen Stadtzentren lebendig zu gestalten. Parallel zu diesen Aufgaben müssen wir auch der Architektur wieder mehr Aufmerksamkeit widmen, denn diese ist ein Teil der Erfolgsgeschichte der Gebäude. Wir dürfen uns dabei auch vor größeren konzeptionellen Anstrengungen nicht scheuen. Wir haben in Berlin beispielsweise mit dem Büro von Renzo Piano zusammengearbeitet, der ja gemeinhin als sehr schwieriger Partner gilt.

———— Otto Riewoldt: Der Geschäftserfolg ist nicht unbedingt von guter Architektur abhängig. In Großbritannien wird der höchste Umsatz pro Quadratmeter am Flughafen in Heathrow erzielt, wo wirklich keine architektonischen Glanzlichter zu bestaunen sind. Die britischen Flughafenbehörden machen heute mehr Geld mit ihren Läden als mit dem Flugverkehr, sechzig Prozent ihres Umsatzes entfallen auf den Einzelhandel.

———— Jens Kalkbrenner: In dieses Geschäft an den Flughäfen sind wir ebenfalls eingestiegen und erzielen dort unglaublich hohe Umsätze.

———— John Hoke: Eine der größten Herausforderungen der Zukunft liegt darin, dass derzeit eine Verbrauchergeneration heranwächst, die nichts davon hält, Dinge allmählich reifen und dann langfristig wirken zu lassen. Was zählt, ist der Augenblick, das sofortige, momentane Erlebnis. Die Kids heute können zwischen Hunderten verschiedenen Fernsehprogrammen herum zappen und mit dem Internet steht ihnen eine Informationsquelle in bis dato unvorstellbarer Größenordnung und Schnelligkeit zur Verfügung. Unsere Herausforderung, das, woran wir in Zukunft arbeiten müssen, sehe ich so: Wir bauen materielle Räume, und diese sollen eine dauerhafte Komponente besitzen, ob das nun ein Jahr, fünf oder 25 Jahre sind. Dennoch sollten sie immer aktuell und unverbraucht bleiben, unmittelbar und direkt wirken. Das ist es, was die Kunden wollen: dass sich ständig etwas verändert. Diese Erwartungshaltung der Kunden an Innovation mit dem Ziel zu vereinbaren, die Innenstädte wieder zu beleben und die historischen Gebäude wieder als Ladenflächen zu nutzen, darin liegt meiner Meinung nach die große Zukunftsaufgabe. Wir wollen unserer Geschäftsidee und Unternehmensphilosophie treu bleiben, brauchen aber zum Brandscaping Räumlichkeiten, die sich rasch und flexibel neuen Bedürfnissen und Anforderungen anpassen lassen.

Der Workshop „Brandscaping – New Dimensions in Retail Design" fand am 27. Juni 2001 im Zumtobel Staff Lichtforum Lemgo statt. Veranstalter waren das Unternehmen Zumtobel Staff und die Architekturzeitschrift DBZ.

Photo Credits / Bildnachweis

Architecture Research Office
97 (2);
BDP Design 25 (1);
BMW 37–39 (12), 41–43 (13),
45-47 (13), 49–51 (10);
Neill Clutton/Arcaid 25–27 (3);
ECE Projektmanagement 55–59
(8), 61–65 (7);
Reid Freeman 101 (1);
David Joseph 97 (left)–99 (4)
100 (1);
Nike 15–21 (17), 26, 28–29 (8);
Markus Pillhofer, Landskrong 5/6,
1010 Wien, Austria 38/39 (1);
RKW Architekten 67–71 (8),
73–77 (8);
Johnson Schwinghammer
97 (right)
Studio Iosa Ghini 81–83 (5),
85–87 (7), 89–91 (6);
Georg Valerius 104–105 (6);
Jos de Vries 93– 95 (10).

Editor | Herausgeber: Otto Riewoldt
Research | Recherche: Ruhmut A. Fenkart
Translation | Übersetzung: Monika Bauer-Boothroyd,
Paul Boothroyd, Otto Riewoldt

The publisher and the editor wish to thank the following
for their kind assistance | Verlag und Herausgeber danken
für die freundliche Unterstützung durch Rat und Tat:
Brigitta van Dijk, Jan Esche, Burkhard Fröhlich, Klaudia Göner,
Andreas Hartweg, Benjamin Hossbach/Phase 1, Jennifer
Hudson, Pat Montgomery, Milena Mussi, Jenny Pollack,
Herbert Resch, Julia Schwärzler, Jochen Stapperfenne,
Sara Thurman, Jos de Vries, Dietmar Zembrot,
Jürg Zumtobel.

A CIP catalogue record for this book is available from the
Library of Congress, Washington D.C., USA.

Deutsche Bibliothek Cataloging-in Publication Data

[Brandscaping - Erlebnisdesign für Einkaufswelten] Brandscaping - Worlds of experience in retail design, Erlebnisdesign für Einkaufswelten / Hrsg.: Otto Riewoldt. - Basel ;
Boston ; Berlin : Birkhäuser, 2002
ISBN 3-7643-6674-5

© 2002 Birkhäuser – Publishers for Architecture,
P.O. Box 133, CH-4010 Basel, Switzerland, and Bertelsmann
Fachzeitschriften GmbH, Gütersloh, Berlin, edition

LICHT
+Architektur

as part of the DBZ Deutsche Bauzeitschrift.
A coorperation in the BertelsmannSpringer Publishing Group
http://www.birkhauser.ch
http://www.fachzeitschriften.ch

Printed on acid-free paper produced from
chlorine-free pulp. TCF ∞
Printed in Germany

ISBN 3-7643-6674-5

9 8 7 6 5 4 3 2 1